BEST CANADIAN POETRY
2020

BEST
CANADIAN
POETRY

2020

GUEST EDITOR: MARILYN DUMONT

SERIES EDITOR: ANITA LAHEY

ADVISORY EDITOR: AMANDA JERNIGAN

BIBLIOASIS
WINDSOR, ONTARIO

FIRST EDITION
ISBN 978-1-77196-364-0 (Trade Paper)
ISBN 978-1-77196-365-7 (ebook)

Series editor: Anita Lahey
Guest editor: Marilyn Dumont
Advisory editor: Amanda Jernigan
Consulting editor: Molly Peacock
Editors at large: Mike Chaulk, Michael Fraser, Laboni Islam,
    waaseyaa'sin christine sy

Cover and text design: Gordon Robertson

 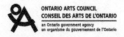

Published with the generous assistance of the Canada Council for the Arts, which last year invested $153 million to bring the arts to Canadians throughout the country, and the financial support of the Government of Canada. Biblioasis also acknowledges the support of the Ontario Arts Council (OAC), an agency of the Government of Ontario, which last year funded 1,709 individual artists and 1,078 organizations in 204 communities across Ontario, for a total of $52.1 million, and the contribution of the Government of Ontario through the Ontario Book Publishing Tax Credit and Ontario Creates.

PRINTED AND BOUND IN CANADA

CONTENTS

FOREWORD

I leave my bird-tracks
in fresh-fallen snow,
and fly away.

— Robyn Sarah, "Artist's Statement"

Each year, as we piece together this anthology, lining up the glories within like specimens of beach glass retrieved from our greedily stuffed pockets, I'm struck anew by the gifts and possibilities poems offer up. I have written in these pages, in past years, of the poem as a home, a safe place to crawl inside; of the poet as investigative journalist with a blessedly creative (and often subversive) twist; of the poem as a "wilderness caught," into which a reader tumbles, ready or not. *Best Canadian Poetry*'s founding series editor, Molly Peacock, has defined and redefined poetry's essential tasks for BCP readers over the years. She once told us, in especially memorable phrasing, that a poem's job is to "articulate the ineffable."

To take the stuff of human existence, intrinsically unsayable, and translate it, score it. Give it words. Now there's a gift.

*

The dark, cold weeks of late winter 2020 were brightened (for me) by several hearty, long-distance consultations with Marilyn Dumont, this edition's guest editor, and BCP's advisory editor Amanda Jernigan, during which we three narrowed down Dumont's longlist of poems. The list began as an impressively tottering heap drawn from Dumont's reading of hundreds of poems, writtsen by Canadian authors, that were published in dozens of print and online journals in 2019. As we read and listened, whittled and mulled, and at last settled those final tough choices, our world veered into pandemic lockdown. April dawned, poetry month, and Biblioasis, *Best Canadian Poetry*'s indomitable publisher (and Windsor, ON's beloved local bookstore), launched an online book club, inviting readers to delve into what, at that time, was the latest BCP: the 2019 edition guest-edited by Rob Taylor. I joined in the first week as a guest, signing into the online platform and seeing my own talking head in a square on the screen amid a dozen or so others. It was my first foray into what has become the meeting "norm" for countless clubs, businesses and organizations during COVID times, and I found it a strange, oddly giddy-making experience, sharing literary chat over this Hollywood-Square-like video grid.

The novelty of the format aside, the poetry commanded our attention. It did its essential work. We delved into poem after poem, our discussion turning, as if inevitably, to the ways each piece spoke to the isolation, uncertainty, fear, and restlessness—and also to the glimmers of hope and joy—that book club members were experiencing. It was a matter of instinct to chart our paths through the poems by the routes that meant most to us on that ordinary Wednesday afternoon, amid what we have all now come habitually to call these extraordinary times.

I emphasize: we didn't reinvent those poems to suit our states of mind. Though they'd first appeared in journals in 2019, and had therefore been completed long before COVID-19, their language, music, and metaphor contained some basic recognition of our plight. Solace was there for the taking.

There's no mystery to this. These were poems: real, hand-made (and handheld) forms built to hold, and simultaneously express, universal truths about the human experience. The wordless things we feel or sense which, in the saying a poem provides, briefly become a *something* we can see, hold, hear, and maybe—for a blink or a flicker—comprehend. Solace was there because the poets who'd written these verses had, by their artful making, worked it in.

*

Dumont's selection is marked by her generosity and warmth, and by her rigour as a reader, and is thereby notably rich in clearly pitched voices, in simple humanity. The gift that comes at me full throttle as I read through these pieces once more, A-to-W by title, is the permission they offer. As we lead lives hemmed in by a host of new rules and public health directives, as permission to engage in so many of the ordinary pleasures and activities of daily life has been rescinded or restricted, it's poetry's nature to *permit* that has me rapt.

Its permissions are vast and ranging. I offer here a few.

To take note.

Of, say, something lost (or never found): "The problem," Alycia Pirmohamed writes in "Avian Circulatory System," "isn't that I don't know my grandmother's first name." "The problem," she writes, "is night—."

Of one of the faces of death: as Babo Kamel writes in "It's Always Winter When Someone Dies," "In the coffin / she looks betrayed, as if caught / doing something she is ashamed of."

Of faint hope: as Nyla Matuk writes in "News Today," "From this fluttering betrayal comes / the weak shadow of a dancing poplar."

To practice devotion: to the divine, to a lover, to home.

"& there are / dreams here under my knees," writes Sanna Wani in "As I pray."

"He searches the garden / for a gift to excite his wife, / and picks a single fig," writes Dell Catherall in "Fig Sestina" (perhaps the sweetest, funniest, sexiest sestina ever composed).

"here on the turtle's back— / on the land of the long white cloud— / home, down under in an endless time of dreaming—," writes Rita Bouvier in "deeper than bone."

To revel—in sound, for starters. See Tanis MacDonald's "Feeding Foxes": "The first listed / ingredient in a bag of pretzels / is puff. So you feed the fox the clever / stuff." Or Kevin Spenst's "It Will Rain Like Rods on the Hillside in Sweden": "It will rain married men in Spain, / and intermittent toads' beards Saturday."

To reinvent (or find?) ourselves: "When I woke up that day I was my grandmother," writes Erín Moure in "Odiama."

To heal, as Rebecca Salazar does (while raging!) in "Poem for unwilling mothers": "Wrap knots of bloodroot / in this page. Steep this pessary / in swamp water to staunch / newly scraped wombs."

To desire. As Jane Eaton Hamilton tells us in "Game Show," "The Earth is lust after all."

To recast—
a place, such as Brandi Bird's in "Selkirk, Manitoba": "The body / of the town a rose bush, a dry thicket"

insomnia, as in Tim Bowling's "3:00 a.m.": "Python swallow. Trying to put / a face to the name of a / truth. One cloud / dissolved by another"

gravity, as in Roger Nash's "Stutters": "For stutterers, Newton got it all wrong. / Unsupported words don't fall / into silence, they just hold their place"

To steal in. "My mother had no room of her own / except the one inside her," writes Maureen Scott Harris in "A Room of My Own."

To zero in, as Jason Purcell does, on "Only the outline of desire around the eye—."

To give in—
    to worry, say, like Margaret Christakos in "Three for One": "Do birds / sleep inside tree trunks? Ball up under / leaf clusters? Tremble in a flock of dark"
    to wind, alongside Jana Prikryl in "Waves": "To walk up the street was to be rinsed"

To note—always and ever, to note. But not to solve, or absolve. I'm out here circling with the birds drawn to the searchlights in Erin Noteboom's "light / cage": "as if to the moon on water."
    Those birds. "once inside our loss / they exhaust themselves in turning."

We—me; the brave Marilyn Dumont; our devoted and profoundly astute advisory editor, Amanda Jernigan; our dedicated team of editors-at-large; and the hard-working crew at Biblioasis, which adapted so swiftly and surely to bookmaking in pandemic times—extend deep gratitude to these poems and their authors, for the permissions they extend.
    We offer those permissions to you.

Anita Lahey
Ottawa, ON
unceded Algonquin, Anishinabek territory

WEIGHT LIFTING

It is February 6th, 2020, and my marriage is falling apart.

I think about tense, as I write this, months later. Is falling? Has fallen. Yes, I think by that time it had certainly fallen, so the present perfect is appropriate, here.

But how about that "has fallen" construction which, if not quite in the passive voice, is certainly passive. Yes, it has a worrying passivity, of the sort against which—avoiding the dangling preposition—I would caution my students.

It is the sort of construction that looks and feels—no, is—evasive.

All right.

It is February 6th, 2020, and I have torn my marriage apart.

I have torn my marriage apart, and it is evening in K'jipuktuk (Halifax) in Mi'kma'ki, and although it is not late in the evening, it is dark. In Ottawa, Algonquin territory, from whence *BCP* series editor Anita Lahey calls me by computer, it is also evening, though perhaps not yet entirely dark. In Amiskwaciy Waskahikan (Edmonton, Alberta), where this year's guest editor, Marilyn Dumont, receives Lahey's phone call, it is early afternoon—as it is also in Wet'suwet'en territory, northwest of there, where just this morning (before daylight) the RCMP moved in to "remove those whose presence would interfere with the lawful execution of duties," as the RCMP press release said.

Remove those whose presence would interfere with the lawful execution of duties: this—to borrow a phrase from Erin Soros's poem at the close of this collection—is what happens to language.

What happens to language is sounding in our ears, then—in my ears, in Anita Lahey's ears, in Marilyn Dumont's ears—as we confer by phone and by computer, to consider Dumont's longlist for *Best Canadian Poetry 2020*. It is sounding in our ears as I read aloud Robert Budde's poem "Blockade," which begins: "dawn, prescient, bulldozer | the flow of resources go also through our mind." It is ringing in our ears as I fraily—oh, how fraily—suggest that there might be an agreement problem in that second phrase.

*

In 2015, Brick Books published a new edition of Marilyn Dumont's debut collection of poems, *A Really Good Brown Girl*, originally published in 1996, as part of its Brick Books Classics series. The introduction to the new edition is by Lee Maracle. Of the original edition, Maracle writes:

> I have kept a copy next to my bed for many years, careful not to damage it in any way. The publishers sent me a new copy, which I promptly lost along with a small suitcase of clothes. I rely on the old one. I read it like it was made of ancient birchbark scrolls, careful not to drink anything near it, spill anything on it. I even wash my hands for thirty seconds before picking it up. I read it every now and then, and it revives me like an old friend.

This is one way to love a book. Another is acknowledged by Dumont herself, who writes in her afterword to the new edition:

Writing these poems not only provided a catharsis for me; they did so for many others who, after readings, approached me with pages of the collection dog-eared. They were often shy and hesitant but grateful that poems like "Leather and Naughahyde" made them feel affirmed in their experience of being Métis. I am humbled that the words I let bleed from me would strike another person who was also made to feel worthless, that the words would buoy someone else's sense of self.

One of my last acts in K'jipuktuk before I fled the city, as the COVID crisis deepened and everyone, everywhere, started washing their hands for thirty seconds all the time—fled, so I could be close to my children, who live in Siknikt, on the Isthmus of Chignecto, in New Brunswick—was to sign out, from the library of Saint Mary's University where I teach English, a copy of that original edition of *A Really Good Brown Girl*. The copy is dogeared ("Half Human / Half Devil (Half-breed) Muse," "The Devil's Language," "The Sound of One Hand Drumming"). Not only that, it is annotated. There are pencilled notes in the margin, written lightly in a loopy hand ("assimilation—new lang/tradition—shame"). Certain passages are underlined—some are underlined and starred. One of those doubly-emphasized passages is this:

> I am in a university classroom, an English professor corrects my spoken English in front of the class. I say, "really good." He says, "You mean, really well, don't you?" I glare at him and say emphatically, "No, I mean really good."

*

the flow of words go also through our mind
    I quote from this year's *BCP*:

> "we'd a fance along, molly, with / a rock in her killick,
> / plimmed and improving by the minute —"

"She asks / about my day about my day about my day"

"Since then wanting / turned into not / wanting to want but wanting / then wanting to want then / refusing to want"

"there is no / word for / benevolent / white men / in my / language"

"'Sometimes' means / daily. 'Body' means / cage. 'Person' means // nothing at all"

"Put down that axe, you ain't / got no bizness messin' with these / roots 'n branches / with the apple of our I"

*

In her poem "pahpowin," Samantha Nock writes:

i keep writing
to create a different world
but i don't know
if you can create worlds
using this language
that is punctuated
with its history
of forced syntax

What happens to language, happens to people.
"What happens" is an evasive construction.
What I do to language, I do to people.
Those whose presence interferes with the lawful execution of duties—are removed.
I can put them back in. "They came in with armed forces to remove peaceful people that are doing the right thing at the right time for the right reasons. We're protecting the land, the air, the water. Our rights and title, our authority as hereditary chiefs. And we're exercising our jurisdiction." That's Na'Moks, a hereditary chief of the Wet'suwet'en Nation, as quoted by CBC News.
What becomes possible in language, becomes possible for people.

What I make possible in language, I make possible for people.

What *these poets,* the poets of *BCP 2020,* make possible in language, they make possible for people. Here is Erin Soros, again:

You work and you wait for the time it waivers, it sinks,
yet you hold it in place, muscle flailing, and this time you
push the weight, your chest's lover that wants to touch
down, you breathe, you breathe again, you raise it higher,
and then higher, with the relish of a man lifting his child
over his shoulders, keeping the metal bar as steady as
a beam tugged up a skyscraper's skeletal new frame.

In this passage, Soros is not just writing about lifting a weight; she is lifting a weight.

Marilyn Dumont is a writer who has taught us how to make things possible for people, by making things possible in language. I can't quite bring myself to dogear the library copy of her 2015 collection *The Pemmican Eaters,* but if I were to do it, this would be the first page I'd turn down:

These Are Wintering Words

Michif problem family among the nuclear language types   one
parent French   the other Cree/Salteaux   wintering words:
sliced thin, smoke-dried, pounded fine, folded in fat and berries
pemmican not pidgin or creole   combining two grammatical
maps   paddle trade routes along waterways   traverse
rapids: white and dangerous with Ojibway women à la façon du
pays   Métis traders, speak la lawng of double genetic origin
pleasure doubled   twice the language   twice the culture
          mixta, not mixed-up, nor muddled   but completely
FrenchCreeOjibway   different tongues   buffalo, a
delicacy source language right from the cow's mouth   mother
of all in-group conversation   wintering camps dispersal

neither Cree, Salteaux nor French exactly, but something else
not less   not half   not lacking

What I find in Marilyn Dumont's *BCP* selection is—not English, exactly; certainly not "the King's English." It is, rather, "something else"—something emphatically *not* less, *not* half, *not* lacking. It is pleasure not doubled but multiplied fifty-fold.

Pleasure, and pain too: for poems are not only, as in Adele Wiseman's wonderful coinage, "joy / Made word." They are also "sorrow / Made word." Joy and sorrow made word, then, wintering—or perhaps springing—among us.

I write this now in May, in Siknikt. Although it is late in the evening, it is still light—light enough that my children can run across the field from their father's, and visit me here, where I write this.

Amanda Jernigan
Mi'kma'ki

INTRODUCTION

Before taking on the task of guest-editing *Best Canadian Poetry 2020*, I had no idea how poems were identified for such an anthology, despite habitually acquiring collections on an annual basis myself. I avidly purchased anthologies throughout the years, and whether I agreed with the anthologist on their yearly selection of poems or not, I always found anthologies instructive because of their capacity to curate a collection of poems that have spoken to a particular poet's aesthetic at a specific time in the literary history of a country. If I consider the number of volumes in my bookshelf with the word "best" in the title, there seems to be no end of the desire to isolate what warrants merit among the genres.

Anthologists are not search engines generating a repository of merit in collections, but instead are human beings pushed and pulled by a plethora of stimuli, praxis, and conceptions of craft while making selections that resonate with them, and thereby, an anthology becomes a record of literary history.

What is a best poem? A best poem fulfills the promise set out in its first syllable, word, syntax, line break, and soundscape to its reader/listener. The work required to complete a poem takes risk, skill and practice, and the poems selected for this anthology all exhibit such attributes.

In my reading criteria, I looked for poems that used language to expose attitudes inherent in the English language itself, the conceptions of civilized/savage; human/nature; sanctioned/forbidden and colloquial/academic. I looked for experimentation in form and approach to content, and gravitated to treatments of topics that were oblique in form. I searched for a poet's control of language as a composer would create a musical score. Some musical scores are lyric, brief and melodic, such as the late Adele Wiseman's "Never Put a Poem Off." Other poetic scores are disruptively cacophonous, such as "Blockade," by Robert Budde; or sustained and sombre, such as the epic score from Erin Soros in "Weight." Prosody is a joyous preoccupation when one comes across poems such as "From Cocks to Wings," by Barry Dempster; "Pink Mints," by Armand Ruffo; or "Stutters," by Roger Nash.

The slant treatment of its topic is what draws me to Robyn Sarah's "Artist's Statement," a clever comment on the ubiquitous required professional biography all poets must craft. "12 Rules for Gatekeeping," by Kyle Flemmer, stood out as a candid list of editorial etiquette seldom shared beyond the pages of a publication. Similarly, I was drawn to the potent illustrative approach taken by Margaret Bollerup in "Dementia and common household objects," which corrals the impenetrable senility, loss of communication, and attendant profound sadness; while Conor Kerr's "Directions to the Culture Grounds" foregrounds cultural difference in simple but brilliant narrative contrast.

Writers of colour, Indigenous writers, women, LGBQT2S writers, writers with physical challenges, have all been underrepresented in the publishing world because, as Daniel Heath Justice has written in his book, *Why Indigenous Literatures Matter* (Wilfrid Laurier University Press, 2018), "assumptions about what is or is not 'literary' are used to privilege some voices and ignore others." So in my deliberation, I was mindful of what Jamaican poet Kei Miller terms the "understory": the narrative that disrupts the falsehoods of benevolence and nationhood. Several selections treat and disrupt settler colonialism and notions of Indigenous deficiency in clever and inventive ways, such as Billy-Ray Belcourt's "Cree Girl Explodes the Necropolis of Ottawa," in which "Nothing / but NDN possibility would flower everywhere outside / the frame"; when Rita Bouvier reminds readers that they are "here on turtle's back" in "deeper than bone"; how Selina Boan unfolds a world of Cree epistemology "Minimal Pairs Are Words Holding Hands"; Samantha Nock's nod to Indigenous resistance through humour in "pahpowin"; Louise Bernice Halfe's "Remember When," which informs readers that the structure of the Cree language does not include the gender binary of "male" and "female" pronouns.

What I didn't anticipate from the task of anthologizing was how this process of selection would reveal to me my own penchant for sarcasm. I was struck with how much my eye is drawn to forms and tones that employ irony, exaggeration, or ridicule to expose and criticize not only individual but collective human folly. I found the subversive desire to challenge collective or self-limiting social norms or taboo around language, belonging, religion, marriage, sex, and gender compelling: these are all subjects of contradiction ripe for satire. This is reflected in chosen poems such as "If I Die Bury Me Next To My Father," by Mugabi Byenkya, the final line of which resonates for both immigrant and Indigenous peoples alike; and "Origin Story," by Kazim Ali, wherein someone is always asking "where are you from"—all stinging indictments of Canada's official multi-culturalism.

I am also drawn to the whimsical in Sadie McCarney's "Bee Funeral" and how its characterization perfectly captures the moodiness of junior high, and Tanis MacDonald's "Feeding Foxes" with its unforgettable image of "Raymond Carver who's running the weed / whacker without noise-cancelling headphones." Likewise, in Fiona Lam's "Ode to the Potato," Lam's focus on the commonplace ubiquitous root vegetable de-familiarizes in the tradition of Neruda. Similarly, Abby Paige in "Hoems," with candor and black humour, generates a poem that reflects the financial realities of a poet.

It's an honour to read the diversity in Canadian poetry and a joy to choose poems that hopefully reflect what others might also consider to be poems that fulfill the promise set out in their first syllable, word, syntax, line break, and soundscape. I am reminded of the late and great Gwendolyn MacEwen's wisdom when she advises us in "Let Me Make This Perfectly Clear" that in matters of poetry, "all you should ever care about / Is what happens when you lift your eyes from this page."

All My Relations,
Marilyn Dumont
amiskwaciy-wâskahikan

Artist's Statement

Robyn Sarah

I do not speak
for the voiceless masses, no.
Nor for the poor, for women, or
for Canada, the True North Strong and Free.
Nor for my other Country 'Tis of Thee.
Not for "my people" (whoever they may be),
nor yet for poets or for poetry.

I do not presume
to speak for anyone but me,
yet hope that speaks for Us.

I "speak." That is to say—
I say what I see, and sus
what I must think is true
from seeing what I say.

It might boil down to *I was here.*

Put differently:
I leave my bird-tracks
in fresh-fallen snow,
and fly away.

— from *Juniper*

As I pray

Sanna Wani

[Islam, / 'ɪslɑːm/; Arabic: "submission, reconciliation, surrender."]

I tap my knees on the ground twice, &
close my eyes (even though they've told me
not to), & the thick fall of my hair has come
undone under my dupata, & I can't tell
where is cloth & where is curl, & there are
dreams here under my knees, under this wood,
beneath this house, & the house built behind it .

I ask my father why he taps his knees,
& he says *not sure*, he says
*I love those dreams even if
I don't understand them*,
& understands what (after all)
but some kind of healing .

then I ask my mother, driving to
Nani's house, & she turns her answer
to the paddy fields, & confesses
*I will never find this kind of forgiveness
anywhere else—*
& forgiveness for what (after all)
but some kind of healing .

one evening, they ask me to recite
a few words of it in the garden,
under the ash tree & the red mountains,
& my knees shatter in their sockets,
& my hair falls from its root,
because I say *no*,
prayer is not a memory,
prayer is a question .

they smile , put my bones back together ,
sew my hair to my scalp , tuck a
curl behind my ear , & say
asking for what (after all)
but some kind of healing .

— from *Canthius*

Avian Circulatory System

Alycia Pirmohamed

Birds have proportionately larger hearts than humans, which is
to say with a heart the relative size

of a crow's to its body, I would need the blood of all my ancestors.

The problem isn't that I don't know my grandmother's first name,
or that I haven't shared the tartness of tamarind

with my mother on any Tanzanian island.

Physiologically, they are so alike: four-chambered, cone and
crescent shaped, but

the problem is night—
how daybreak transforms two identical stones into a motherland

and a daughter, depending on the snarl of grassland at their ankles.

I have spent too long wishing for the heart of something else,
bathing in a pond

in secret, so that I might hide the lacquer of my anatomy. I envy
birds that pump blood according to instinct,

never concerning themselves with the bloodline threading
through.

— from *The Fiddlehead*

Bee Funeral

Sadie McCarney

In fifth grade Crybaby and Almost-
Boobs hoarded curios in a Kleenex
box: hunks of rock shaped like
pizza slices, gel pens' worn-out

tips. Crud. That summer behind
the dugout they found the body:
like seppuku, the bumblebee had
stung itself dead. So Crybaby

and Almost-Boobs became funeral
directors. From their Kleenex box
they got a monogrammed hankie
for its shroud, its coffin a torn-up

tarot box from Almost-Boobs' Wiccan
babysitter. Crybaby held in her aquifer
of tears even though it almost geysered
(like when she forgot her lunch, or

fell down). But what would a bee need
to pack like a sack lunch, for whatever
might be coming after? Crybaby gave
it flowers: a broken dollar-store lei,

daisy stickers, a stemless silk rose.
For a marker, Crybaby and Almost-
Boobs suckled pink Popsicles, made
a cross with the sticks. That Fall

Almost-Boobs became Boobs. She
began to date Boyfriend 1, quit their

Kleenex box full of tinsel and crud.
Crybaby cried. The bumblebees flew.

— from *Literary Review of Canada*

Blockade

Rob Budde

dawn, prescient, bulldozer | the flow of resources
go also through our mind | cardboard boxes
and broken crates on fire; three white-tails further down the
ditch | first, what family's land | the
road, the pipe, the terminal, the tanker, the destined port,
the profit—all going away and leaving | resting
crouched on the ground, feet planted, listening to the sounds
of small creatures, the air, the rich smell of *Hoolhghulh*
powering the ravine, the trickle of water everywhere, the place
is not numbers, the place is not yours | a tourniquet
would seem so enticing too | enbridging v. : to
make a leap in logic that dismisses all other points of view
| nation-building" the minister's claim staked |
what else is a 1991 Civic for | named Tehwehron,
named MacBlo Brutalist in 1993 | this passive act
of war, this bodied word | lyric line = pipe line

crossroads, a gas station, and a tow truck overturned |
the joint review panel should have gone and sat in the woods
for three days instead | a 50-metre right-of-
way through vital organs | Tiananmen Square
1989: "It is necessary to take a clear-cut stand against distur-
bances" | paved with state-of-the-art technology
| an overseas market compass | a 100
meter wave in 1977 | all a history of the roads in
| what type of line is created, how is it traversed, and
to what end | built up junctures split |
standing in front of a large machine is not blocking prog-
ress | the time it takes to get a sticky price tag off
something | an act of creation in standing one's
ground | the storied land is waiting dormant

| there is this wise saying that has almost been forgotten
| he 10% equity offer hung in the air like smog |
occupy the health of a place |

| you were there, sewing patches for strength |
a knack for being in the wrong place and a disregard for per-
sonal safety | can't stop can't slow can' give can't
care can't live can't recant can't not can't | by
the sign saying 'watching for trucks turning', by the sign that
something is awry | the territory's family name
| sub-boreal spruce and balsam: *picea* speaking outside
the frame | the result not conclusive, but the
intervening language moved back south | what
is it about the interruption of the normal? | wild
rose cattail soapberry and raspberry | the first
bulldozer here 1969 under Socreds | gravel
from Chetwynd | asphalt | centre
line | is the message delivered or stopped?
| flows and systemanalysis concluded that the excess
was not accounted for | LNG is fracked gas and
the quakes are just starting

| an oily patch on the way | the BC Access
Office is where you renew your driver's license |
a prepositional phase | the reason for the
media is a place to record the movement of public emo-
tion | can't go, further | a stop in a
line of energy, when | as if the self was yours to
throw in front of | the pit house slept up to 12
| municipal, provincial, or federal policy finds your
local, assumes | of first traditional |
if Delgamuulk is ignored | a trap set at each
blueprinted line | an ally does the work, asks no
reward | an eagle feather Promise |
TransCanada changes its name to TC Energy to lower

Google hits | lives cut hereditary and Indian
Act | it would say that story doesn't belong on
this land | when being a polite host fails |
3rd phase of the Healing Centre's concrete base

— from *The Goose*

clumper crackies/Ice Pan Puppies

Geoff Pevlin

clumper crackies

we'd a fance along, molly, with
a rock in her killick, plimmed
and improving by the minute—
handy on to peasing all over
the ice—when just apass noon
a chinker wee-gees in the floe
inside of us and the beaver-
hat-man, and we rushed back
towards the ship after seeing the
dark streaks of open seawater
on the white surface of the pan.

The crack was close on ten feet
at first and a strong storm kicked
up into our faces, gristly snow
pounding down as darkness
descended around us. Old Molly
sprinted ahead, ending up on a
loose ice-pan and floated away,
driven off and disappeared like a
fetch back on to the ice blink—a
right lumper and I'm hardly
blowing the roast to chaw on
about how chummy the crew
bees with the canines.

but, by the man, nar wrinkle,
she marled upalong the next
marn after whelping on the
same sheet she took off on like a
right saddleback—every puppy
handsome and healthy as a two-
masted vessel in a steady breeze.

Ice Pan Puppies

We'd a dog with us, Molly, who
was pregnant, swelling more by
the minute—close on to bursting
all over the ice—when sometime
in the afternoon a crack formed
between us and the ship, and we
scravels directly after scunning
the smutty dunduckity drent of
open brine on the googy-egged
barrens.

the slatch was nar ten feet, first
going off, a right sustained
sheila in our features, gristy
snow fluxxing down, coming on
duckish nowda once. and auld
molly forelayed us on the ree-
raw, ending up on a brickled off
floe, disappearing like a phantom
ship with her back facing the
glow of a distant sheet. This was
tragic. I'm not revealing any
secrets to talk about how much
the whole crew loved our dogs.

But, by God, not a word of a lie,
she floated back to us the next
morning after giving birth right
there on the same sheet of ice she
left on just like a seal would—all
paws clever and jonnick as a
jackass brig in a mad shuff.

— from *The Fiddlehead*

The Clean Language List

Don Kerr

as a member of the clean language list
he said holy smoke and gee whiz
he said jesus like in jesus made me
to know him and love him
thought they'd never met or he said
hell as in hell fire which is where
he was going the scary fire
eating the air while his father
paid a nickel a swear and he and his
sister became the administrators of
the foul language institute local 220
once, working at a Canada Dry plant,
he discovered at last what fuck meant,
well, he said to himself, fuck that,
fuck me, fuck you, could have given
a fortune in nickels were there only
a member of the clean language list
there to clean up

— from *Grain*

Cree Girl Explodes the Necropolis of Ottawa

Billy-Ray Belcourt

In the first seven minutes of Jeff Barnaby's *Rhymes for Young Ghouls*, Anna (Roseanne Supernault) kills herself and who but her daughter, Aila (Devery Jacobs), is left to witness her body suspended in thick air. "The day I found my mother dead, I aged one thousand years," she says from the future. Aila goes on to take the helm of a drug-dealing business and to seek revenge against the Indian agent who erodes with vicious precision the social worlds of those living on the reserve. If I were to make a short film, it would be about a Cree girl who builds a time machine fuelled by the feeling power of rez dogs. She would obliterate herself and be born anew in a year in which one could be a Cree girl and desire a world outside the field of vision of what are now two ministries of NDN misery. In fact, the opening sequence would be shot via a hand-held camera as the Cree girl explodes the necropolis of Ottawa. Nothing but NDN possibility would flower everywhere outside the frame. That is, the film would not be about the bloodied hands of history nor what it is to be an object of sorrow in the eyes of both the reconciler and the executioner. Instead, we would see only the Cree girl through a low-angle shot, and at no point would she be anything but a cartographer who maps a world in her image and no one else's.

— from *Prairie Fire*

deeper than bone

Rita Bouvier

when they ask you
who are your people?
say...

they are the people
who live

    in the clearing where the rivers empty
    in the narrows of beaver river valley
    in haida gwaii
    at the foot of the three sisters

they are the people
who live

    along the bay of winipakw
    along the river where bow reeds grow
    along the valley of the grande riviere
    on top of small mountain

they are the people
who live

    where two rivers come together
    where the people fish
    where the humpback salmon spawn
    near the lizard's domain

they are the people
who live

    by the waterfall place
    by the holy springs
    by the strait of the spirit
    in the place of peace

here on turtle's back—
on the land of the long white cloud—
home, down under in an endless time of dreaming—
the coming together, the falling apart
as it is today and forever.

— from *Grain*

Dementia and common household objects

Margret Bollerup

Now we talk in tiny circles. She asks
about my day about my day about my day
and I tell her something new each time
every time so I am not
caught in this loop, so my voice
does not go thready, does not
grow swollen with impatience.

She tells me again again about
how she and her friends she and her friends
went to that restaurant because it was some
one's birthday, and hers, and that was nice.
It was someone's birthday. And the restaurant
the restaurant was nice. Someone's
birthday. Hers.

I say, how nice, how nice
that it was nice. That restaurant
is nice. How are her friends. Whose
birthday was it, besides hers. I'm so glad
it was nice.

And she asks about the dog, the dog,
how is my dog, hers are good,
the new one scruffy, the new one
pushing at the old one, and scruffy.
The dogs not getting along,
and how is my dog.

And I say she's fine, my dog,
and I'm glad hers are fine. My dog,
I say, is fine

but has started to whine when I lie
on the couch and try try and try
to hold myself
      my shards the edges stinging sharp
together.

But I don't say that part.
That part unsaid
and unsaid
and unsaid.

— from *The New Quarterly*

Directions to the Culture Grounds

Conor Kerr

Social Worker Version
(as recited through the telephone and then sent in an email
for confirmation).

Drive west on the Whitemud, keep going when it turns into
    Hwy 628
Turn left on Hwy 60
Turn right on Twsp 523
Turn left at red pylon
They can't make it though, busy doing paperwork.

(as recited through the telephone, no email confirmation).

Head straight out past the River Cree heading west until you hit the edge of the reservation. Turn left and go down until you see Oskya on the righthand side of the road, just past Joe's old trailer. Watch out for RCMP they're always out on that road. Drive past the Cardinal sign on the lefthand side of the road. They haven't thrown any water down on the road in a few years and the dusts really been kicking up so watch out for dogs. Go past my Nokhums shack, where I was raised. Turn left at that orange pylon. Follow the ruts down the trail, unless the boys have brought gravel and filled them in. In that case, follow the gravel. Either way follow the trail back into the birch trees past the family of prairie chickens crushing gravel into their gizzards. Don't shoot any, those are my chickens. You leave those chickens alone. Go past the gate, you might have to move it. It's dummy locked and it will swing once you work the rust out of the hinge. Hasn't swung well for about 10 years. So you'll need to give it a good pull for encouragement. On the right side you'll see faded yellow, red, and white prints hanging in the trees. Those are from our family my boy. Though you may have never met them they put those there for you. If you can hear the magpies squawking your arrival you'll be at the right place. You'll see the old sundance lodges where the boss tree still stands strong even though everything else has gone back to the land. There's a little shack with a tin roof surrounded by piles of those good lava rocks, the ones from Clearwater, and river rocks, and rocks that have cracked. Some old green and blue tarps, getting pretty holey so we've doubled them up on the chopped birch. Don't look at that green cut birch, it still needs to find its place. Another shack, this one circular with a rusted out stove pipe coming out the roof, will be farther back past the next strand of birch and willow trees and the grass field. Hopefully the boys have cut that grass by now, was getting pretty long. There should be smoke coming out of that chimney. Come inside, we'll be waiting for you.

— from *The Malahat Review*

Feeding Foxes

Tanis MacDonald

A starfish has no brain. Ospreys fledge atop
hydro poles in nests big as tractor tires. Pain

is relative: my aunt lived until ninety
on microwaved soup. She used to say, *The more*

you feed foxes, the faster they turn into dogs.
You're so clever and quick. Are you roaming

the schoolyard, spoiling for a fight? Are you on fire?
Are you taking the onramp too fast? Are there

three dead possums on the roadside in no-evil-
monkey poses: hands over head, hand on heart,

face down? A red line of ants streams towards them,
close harmony, love's sweet seam. Some days you

will be strolling a meadow beside the field
of cultural production; you'll have to hide

from Raymond Carver who's running the weed
whacker without noise-cancelling headphones.

He can't hear himself cough. Who taught you to
laugh like a drain, to walk the plank of your

planetary platform? The first listed
ingredient in a bag of pretzels

is puff. So you feed the fox the clever
stuff. Speak low, vote often; you're sly enough.

— from *Contemporary Verse 2*

Fig Sestina

Dell Catherall

A breath of cloud purples
a hot August eve.
He searches the garden
for a gift to excite his wife,
and picks a single fig,
aged to perfection.

Hard to keep a perfect
fruit that's matured to purple.
Roosting crows peck at figs
on a summer's eve;
he yells like a fishwife
and slings nuts into the garden.

Is his fruit from The Garden?
Who's to say Adam's perfect
temptation for swiving
was red. Why not purple?
A woman as reckless as Eve
would crave a fig.

His wife doesn't give a fig
for a Mac from the garden.
On their anniversary eve
she knows an imperfect
world will bruise purple
patches in everyone's life.

Her husband, long wifed
confidently figures
she harbours purple
imaginings in the garden.

He considers her body perfectly
delicious, though long past Eve's.

She flaunts sagging flesh on the eve
celebrating 45 years of wifely
devotion, knowing imperfections
incite love. The fragile skinned fig
mirrors her gardener,
as sensitive as the colour purple.

He cuts evenly through the ripe fig,
offering his wife the love he's gardened;
she bites into perfection and tastes purple.

— from *The New Quarterly*

From Cocks to Wings

Barry Dempster

Spring in Central Park's Tavern on the Green

This year's orchids are in situ,
keeping their tiny cocks covered,
bashful amidst the greenhouse
array of showy body parts.
They belong to the same grandeurs
as raindrops pearling on swathes
of satin-April grass, powdered trunks
of ghostly birch, *xanthoria parietina*,
a shade of lichen so inimitably yellow,
Tiffany's has yet to duplicate it.
Even flukes dazzle: mushrooms
lined up for luncheon like hats
in a rich man's closet; ferns
still learning how to chill; pine cones
hanging on by just one sticky drop.
We could praise Nature for days,
like statues gushing water
from their marble mouths. When orchids
bluster into bloom, the transformation
of cocks into wings, that leap from sex
to spirit, never fails to astound,
the maître d' of precious apparatus
restoring us to metaphor's full five senses.

— from *Grain*

Game Show

Jane Eaton Hamilton

I think I know what death is
you say, but things that seem dead are not dead
in the morning, or in springtime. Springtime
happens more often than you
would expect. It happens at least
once a year. It flutters its name:
Narcissus. The Earth is lust after all
Admire my boulders. Climb my mountains
Settle in my trees. Bathe in my cavities. Hover above me
The Earth has more experience in lust than we ever will
Look at all the babies she had: *axolotls,* for criminy's sake
In this house, things that seemed dead
are not dead in the morning
the daffodils lift on their stalks
crazed with yellow
my mother in the shadows smokes her final
cigarette never imagining her end
came years ago
In this house, even your weird father is alive again
Look! Women kneel around him, massaging his feet
the flowers in their coiled hair wilting and reviving
seven times, seventy times
Ghosts, I say,—*not always spectral*
No, you say, *I think I've figured it out*
It's just the damned zoosia again, and
the cat is still starving. Can't you help her?
The shadow cat growls under the table
her stomach destroyed
from opioids, just as in life. The lesson
might be: Suffering is long
everyone must get the pain to end
one way, or, yes, the far better way, with life

The cat abruptly rises, grooms
with her cancerous tongue—
If I touch tender on her
somatosensory cortex her tumours shrink
her tongue unsticks from the valley of her jaw
She vanishes anyhow. *Is that what you mean?*
Sometimes in this game show, you lift a table leg
and it is just a table leg, set improperly, wobbling
but sometimes you move it to
your mouth to discover it's cake
You say you love me. I say *I love you*
I want serenity and safety, same as anyone
(the run-on sentence where we are in this together)
I dream you are dead. There's a light
inside your body. You stand
in the living room for me to read by
Pink snow falls softly on our shoulders
on the feather quilt
insisting springtime, and we hold hands—
or we hold hands, insisting springtime, so
our hair breaks into cherry bloom

— from *The Puritan*

Selected Hoems

Abby Paige

Checkbook   unbalanced
broke   or broken
breadwinner   breadloser

the poetics of housework
work written on water
erasure as publication

sometimes it feels like
I'm fighting this battle
against the Tupperware drawer
all alone.

the domestic labour
that purchased
the silence
that wrote every poem
that you've ever read

No one looks into my eyes as frequently
or fervently as the food in the freezer.

The crack	between
cupboard	and stove
where the	offal goes
forgive that	crack in me

The bodies, the antibodies
The fluids, the family
A semblance, resemblance
All the belly buttons in the house

I don't know how they sliver almonds
or the sunset, I vaguely remember
how late is Safeway open?
a lifetime ago

— from *Arc Poetry Magazine*

If I Die Bury Me Next To My Father

Mugabi Byenkya

One grave over from Jajja Musajja
One grave up
from the
One foot grave
of the
One month old cousin I never got to know

We're gonna have to clear more trees around the family
    graveyard soon
because death trails my family like the police trail me

Walking through my neighbourhood as they ask—
me:
(neighbourhood resident of three years)

my brother:
(neighbourhood resident of six years)

"What are you doing in this neighbourhood?"

Have you ever felt homeless in your own home?

    — from *Juniper*

It Will Rain Like Rods on the Hillside in Sweden

Kevin Spenst

It will rain married men in Spain,
and intermittent toads' beards Saturday
morning in Portugal. An intense
Pacific frontal system of bamboo
grass and sand will fall over Tokyo.
There's a chance of young cobblers
developing over Berlin and running
riot across the country all the way
to Athens, where they will fall
Sunday afternoon alongside chair legs.
In Nantes, it's currently raining
nails, in Grenoble its *grenouilles*,
ropes in Reims, and Niort is
getting nailed. Cows are pissing
lightly over Paris. In the north
of Taipei, plums will plummet Monday morning.
There's a strong chance of fire
and sulfur over Reykjavík, which
will reek of burnt umbrellas for weeks.
In Bangkok, it will rain
children's eyes and ears shut for a month,
and then they will open and be quizzed
like little gods on all the winds in the sky.

— from *Taddle Creek*

It's Always Winter When Someone Dies

Babo Kamel

New snow
Mother's high heeled boots track
a path to nowhere.

In the coffin
she looks betrayed, as if caught
doing something she is ashamed of.

*

Winter in Montreal, so cold
your nostrils stick together
on those long walks after storms.

Once Peter, lost in his own good looks
rang my doorbell to celebrate
the first snow. I think now

it was only some romantic
version of himself that led him to my front door
a snowflake riding his lash.

*

Years later he showed up after Father's funeral,
wearing knee high boots, smoking non-stop
declaring cancer scare a farce.

Back from the cemetery, where an old woman stood in the cold
palm out asking
something for the living?

We sat on low wooden chairs in the living room
where for years, my father slept, and drank himself
as far as he could get from my mother's death.

So strange to be in that room, his paintings
        on the wall, brilliant and brooding,
brushstrokes as intimate as breath.

— from *Contemporary Verse 2*

Kris Knight, The Flying Monkey, 2014.
Oil on canvas, 24 x 18 inches.

Jason Purcell

Only the outline of desire around the eye—
something I might orient myself toward, that might
direct my body into collision with other bodies.
I wanted it once: in junior high, the invitation
to warm the body of another
boy who was only cold underneath his jeans, who knew
my mouth was the hottest part of me.
But then he let the story go
through the school like a flood
wetting the hems of my pants with shame.
None of the girls would touch me
during dance class. Since then wanting
turned into not
wanting to want but wanting
then wanting to want then
refusing to want now
the outline of it around the eye
petals fanning outward and my pupil
where its sex would be if it had any.

— from *Prairie Fire*

light/cage

Erin Noteboom

Every year on September 11th, eighty-eight searchlights
line the foundations of the fallen towers,
and push their hollow shapes as tall
as light can reach. I say "hollow"
because the lights also make a cage
that captures birds. A hundred thousand sometimes, baffled
by the beams they take for solid. Migrating,
they are drawn as if to a smacking window,
as if to the moon on water, and once inside our loss
they exhaust themselves in turning, in making the beams
flash with wings as white as moth or mirror. We know this.
We know it before we turn them on, these towers made of gauze.
And we know them, the birds—the beauty and the cost.

    — from *Prairie Fire*

louise

Dallas Hunt

nôhkom nitânskotapân
was born
with one
eye
and one
kid-
ney

for her grandchildren
she worked
her brittle fingers
into dough,
into the edges
of fires,
into frost-lined
canopies,
into dust she'd
knead with
flour and
bake for
us awâsisak

"bannock weighs
heavy on bones,"
she'd say,
and lick the
lard from fingers
that cracked with
love and life
for ancestors that
linger,
welcomely, and
for the

ancestors
to come

for white men,
nôhkom nitânskotapân
has awâs
tattooed on her
knuckles,
back hunched,
vigilant, yet
carrying herself
with that
looseness of being
that glides on,
and with,
the wind

nôhkom nitânskotapân
strikes with the
fury of
a thousand
aunties,
whispering
"there is no
word for
benevolent
white men
in my
language"

— from *Contemporary Verse 2*

nôhkom nitânskotapân: my great grandmother.
awâsisak: children
awâs: go away

Minimal Pairs Are Words Holding Hands

Selina Boan

kisik (and also)
kisik she texts, *it's refreshing*, dating a girl who doesn't want to
     talk every day.
It's been two months since I walked concrete in platform
     shoes and my heart still hurts.

kîsik (the sky)
Sometimes love is a question in my underwear drawer and
     the way bracelets sound in air.
It is a blue mirror and the way the world listens through kîsik.

Pisiw (a lynx)
I watch my roommate move the earth of one plant to another
     in the sink.
She tells me her dreams. The pisiw she saw in the alley on her
     way to a party, her hair burning.

Pêsiw (bring someone)
Pêsiw to your ex's wedding who speaks their mind and
     reminds you this is why laughter exists.
Who knows your holding-everything-in-eyes means, you
     don't want a hug. Speeches on fire.

Niya (me/1)
This summer is a planet and the yous in this poem are exes,
     missing family, general advice, niya.
This summer is a house party. Overhearing someone say, that
     native girl, she was so *well-spoken*.

Niyâ (lead/go ahead)
You niyâ me to the place they found his body. Your own body
     a lit window, a quiet x-ray.
Words vibrate worlds if you listen.

Niyanân (us)

I never took a photo with my birth dad, hold niyanân
    together in my mind. His face in mine.
Days fit into the holes where my wisdom teeth once were.
    Blood nerve.

Niyânan (five)

I made a fire. Missed knowing nohkom in this world by
    niyânan years.
Missed getting the Nêhiyawêwin right in this poem, words
    stitched together and growing.

Sakahikan (a nail, for building)

In grade six, I snuck a small tin of blue eyeshadow to school.
    Fingers blue from touching myself.
I kept the things I thought I'd need in a jar: the feet of yellow
    tights, sakahikan, elastic bands.

Sâkahikan (a lake)

My mother's microwave doesn't have time, just two neon dots
    stacked and blinking.
There is so much dust on her bathroom blinds, it forms a
    sâkahikan. A soft universe in horizontal.

Kona (snow)

Outside Esso, kona starts rounding itself up in my ears. The
    world gone side-ways.
When anxiety stretches itself up into your body, look around
    and ask yourself, are you safe?

Pona (put it in the fire)

You slept in a sleeping bag, rolled your jacket into its own
    hood and prayed it wouldn't rain.
Tonight, pona. Star guts and the space between your fingers
    where night appears.

Ôma (this)

Today, my heart is a staircase. I am incapable of the love others deserve.

Ôma is my apology. A gas station on the way to visit my father. The room you and I once shared.

Ôta (here)

Isn't it funny how we can remember and forget at the same time?

Ôta, where we first hold hands, become the mouths words camp inside, for a while, at least.

— from *Room*

Never Put a Poem Off

Adele Wiseman

Never put a poem off
It's a vain, capricious thing
You may put off eating
You may defer play
You may even, briefly,
Put your love away
But ask a flash of verse to wait
Till you find pencil, pen or slate,
In vain,
You'll never see that joy
Made word again.

— from *Juniper*

News Today

Nyla Matuk

A lamplit walk
to the ocean
and tidal influence

following rumour, mirage—
the longed-for mercy ship
that never arrives

and the year just getting started,
as we like to point out.

Seafoam, that crabbed allure,
seen and heard along the byroad
transfiguring with the crescent waning,
came and went with a natural
constancy, a dynamism.
Against this, we go to make our visit.

We observe the usual sallying forth springing on
the displaced surface, then hummingbirds who
beat their wings in wallpapery delight toward morning.

From this fluttering betrayal comes
the weak shadow of a dancing poplar,
its charm and hush notes always a single flat
or sharp away from the margin.

We carry hope of crossfire
drawing from the body of water,
for a piece of evidence

checked absolutely
for evidence.

— from *The Walrus*

Ode to the Potato

Fiona Tinwei Lam

On the table's altar,
roast beasts and ornate sweets
might claim the limelight.
But for you we labour
through the necessary ablutions,
scraping skin, gouging out
imperfection to reveal
your pearly flesh.
Stalwart one, you cushion
against famine's edge
with the reprise of storied feasts,
steaming clouds
crowned with molten gold.

One afternoon, I plunged
my hands in dirt, seeking
your lumps of rosy, tawny treasure.
Soul of the soil, how you gleamed
in the dark loam as if deities
had transformed stones to sate
the hungers of the world.
Gazing up at me, your many eyes
that quested in darkness
for moisture, mineral, sun.

— from *The New Quarterly*

Odiama

Erín Moure

after rereading C.D. Wright's "The Obscure Lives of Poets"

When I woke up that day I was my grandmother
her long brown hair falling to her shoulders
the day she had it cut
and after that wore
pincurls

her eyes of the hill and farmyard
she was a lady of Ukraine
her father had a cow
her husband was a blacksmith's apprentice

already one step to the urb of the future
where he made not horses' shoes or hasps for doors
but shells
for American cash registers
and pigs at River Furnace
for American steel

The urb of the future
already one step toward the urb of the internet
where every person has their own cash register
and river on fire
and their own *passé composé*
and their own *dyakuyu*

her skin
my grandmother's skin and steadfast gaze that was the eyes of
    the skin
now I have this skin I must adopt this look too

I am a lady of Ukraine and don't you forget it
solitary
as a step of a cow in the mud of a farmyard in the lee of a hill in
        Ukraine where the sun
only hits later in the day and so the hoofprint
dammit
just stays there

my grandmother is so long dead this entire *torque* is useless
I can't call it a p--m so I call it a *torque*

to hell with you

my grandmother never would have said that
she wished damnation's torment on no one, even an enemy
for her enemies she was just sad
but I can't be sad for my *torque* only maybe angry a bit

for me it is not yet time I do not think
for pincurls

whatever

not even a rosary
not even a wooden bench
not even a pump for water in the lean-to of my first Western home

suddenly I realize it is me the urb of the future
a woman's body
hurtled forward out of the step of the cow by my grandmother
long ago
right past my mother when she wasn't looking
right past the pigs and cash registers of her burning husband
right across the Cuyahoga River stunk with industry into
the high birches of the Dane-zaa and bushes of berries

harbouring forever the face
the texture of her face
a skin that finally
—after an apprenticeship to voyages and husband and the ocean
of stars over Ukraine—
one line at a time
having arrived at my face
learned
speaking

Erín Moure
Glascott, Ontario, Canada
Meridian: 80°46'40"W

Came out with her little arms windmilling through the waiting people and
once past them quietly lifted the latch up and went outside (light blinding)
and sat beneath a tree.

— from *Arc Poetry Magazine*

Origin Story

Kazim Ali

Someone always asks me "where are you from"
And I want to say a body is a body of matter flung
From all corners of the universe and I am a patriot
Of breath of sin of the endless clamor out the window
But what I say is I am from nowhere
Which is also a convenience a kind of lie

When I was sitting in the Mumbai airport this January
On a forty hour layover rushing home because
My mother had had a stroke and could not speak
I wondered about my words
Perhaps I am from my words
Because the basic biography is ordinary

Born in Croydon to a mother and a father who
On different sides of a national border
Were married in war time and had to reunite in England
The only place they could both get to
Born at home—76 Bingham Street
Midwived and not doctored into the world

Taken back to India when the war was over
Where I came into language and of the seven
That were spoken in the house I began speaking four as the
    same
Then to the cold Canadian north we went to a town that no
    longer exists
On the other side of Cross Lake from the Indians
Who lost everything because of the dam my father was
    helping to build

Then to Winnipeg then to New York City
Then to Buffalo
Which I can claim
I can say I am from Buffalo because
It is a city of poets
The city of Lucille Clifton

I arrive there in cold January to find my mother
A little slowed down but still self-possessed enough
To cook meals for everyone
Even if she didn't remember the names of all the spices she
        was using
She talks by the time I arrive but slowly and deliberately
And she has to listen very carefully to be able to respond

She pauses while she talks and cocks her head while she thinks
She does not criticize me nor say anything about my wild hair
Our ordinary silence does not seem as suffocating
Because I wait patiently while she strains to find each word
And what on earth does it mean that
I almost like my mother better this way

When my mother went to her medical appointment
I got out my copy of *good woman* and combed through its lines
To find the addresses where Lucille grew up and lived
I climb into the car with a map and a journal and drive
Through the snow to find those places and take photographs
Of the empty lots where the houses once stood

Listen:
I have no answer to your question
I am not kidding when I tell you:
I earned my own voice

The shape it makes in the world holds me
I have no hometown no mother tongue

I have not been a good son

— from *The Fiddlehead*

pahpowin

Samantha Nock

i wonder if it's disrespectful
to be depressed
on someone else's territory

cree cackles
are the melody
to halfbreed sadness
can this land
hold us
wholly

i keep writing
to create a different world
but i don't know
if you can create worlds
using this language
that is punctuated
with its history
of forced syntax
how many more
moniyawak
are going to tell me
i'm so well spoken

growing up we learned
from kokum
to tell a dirty joke
and follow it with
your saddest confession

i'm not so well-spoken
on the phone
with my mom
when the northern crawls out
and i slip back into
the belonging

i tried not to belong to
when i went to university
because the rich white boy down the hall
made jokes that i grew up in a trailer park
not that there's anything wrong with a trailer park
but i didn't want to tell him that
even his white boy imaginations of poverty
were so far off

> i laugh well
> i laugh futures into existence
> i laugh loud
> and energetic
> because this existence is funny
> deeply ironic
> and unexpected

in highschool social studies
we had to write a paper on if
louis was a sane or insane

looking at pictures of your kin
listening to your teacher
who smells like dust
and colonialism
tell you that louis was:
a murderer
a crazy murderer
a crazy treasonous murderer

i grew up with louis's picture next to jesus's
and i say that he was the leader of us
i get a C-
i didn't know what a heretic is

> the future is
> aunties sitting
> a kitchen table
> laughing

and drinking tea
and swearing
because we survived
and got to make a joke of it.

— from *PRISM international*

Pegging Out Washing

Frances Boyle

The indoor line
dries sullen, planks jeans,
towels are sandpaper, sheets standoffish,
socks stunted shells. Cotton needs motion
to dry to softness.
                            But the dryer grumbles
with noise and static, things cling
or are perfumed fluorescent.

Today you crave
the outdoors. You lug the load,
damp in basket, to the yard, and peg
shadows of legs, arms, echoes of feet.
Wind-channeled sunshine,
breath of breeze wins over, moisture
exhales.
            Fabric yields
to drape shoulders, skirts swirl in soft pleats, buttons
slide out of buttonholes. T-shirts nuzzle
like jersey. Sheets billow and fill,
brush your face, wrap hips, shins.

Their touch is shivery.

— from *Queen's Quarterly*

Pink Mints

Armand Garnet Ruffo

They're in the kitchen laughing. I'm on the couch half
watching the hockey game. Saturday night, and Mervin
is making up my mother. He applies some red lipstick and
digs into his black case and takes out a small paint brush.
He dips it into a small container and brushes her cheeks.
My mother is wearing her sparkly blue dress and black
high heels that match her black hair. Mervin's wearing a
tight white shirt, yellow socks, pointed shoes and black
slacks, the dress up kind I wear on special occasions.

When I was younger Mervin used to babysit me and other
kids from the neighbourhood. He'd take us to the movie
theatre where he'd give us brooms we'd push around like
a little army. He'd let us keep any money we found, and
we'd stick our thin arms between the seats feeling for coins.
If we behaved ourselves, at the end of the job he'd stick his
arm behind the locked candy counter and slip out a package
of mints.

He always grabbed the pink ones. We preferred them any-
ways. The white ones burned our mouths. We'd stand in a
row, and Mervin would drop a mint on our tongues just like
Communion. Tonight they're going to The Sportsman's
Lounge or maybe to a party. I tell them to have a good time,
and go back to the hockey game and don't think anything.
That will come later from the snickers of the kids at school.
Where I'll float above myself and act like I don't know him.

— from *The Malahat Review*

Poem for unwilling mothers

Rebecca Salazar

Embroider white cushions
with nests of hair pulled
from the semen-clogged drain.

Stain the mattress every cycle.
New blood pools new relief
maps: a lunar topography
outlines still-nameless craters.

The ragged spaces in this poem
silhouette you dangling
a newborn aloft by the ankle.

It spells an anagram of every name
you've chalked across the floor
to summon daughters you won't have.

It nuzzles your breast, raising
delicate folds like the scalded milk-skin
you'll dissect with the blade
of a spoon.

It asks if you can hear the ticking.

It will birth itself, choking
and noosed with wet cords,
a stray spool-shuttle snared in the loom.

Wrap knots of bloodroot
in this page. Steep this pessary
in swamp water to staunch
newly scraped wombs.

Re-engineer the cogs burst
from your biological clock
into a pipe bomb,

and smudge your face while burying
this poem in that ravine
where tiny skeletons are found.

— from *Room*

The Process of Growth

Ashley Hynd

they say identity is about who claims you
not just the blood in your veins—but being
lost and found is subsequential—if no one knows
you are missing
                does anyone go look for you

*   *   *

                        my brother beats drum
                        outside the AGO 150
                (plus 10,000-15,000 truths)

                      tells me I don't understand
                    if I had seen what he has seen
                    I'd bring them drugs too

*   *   *

in the dream I was the cross
Jesus bled upon my forehead
fox was a mocking bird
screaming
          nothing
               nothing
                    nothing

in the morning, mould crept
between my toes grew into ivy

wrapped round his feet
whispering

        reclaim

            reclaim

                reclaim

when the clouds came
the sun gave way
to his salt and ash   sweat

        I will smell like this
        two thousand years
        later

        when Madonna
        burns me

*   *   *

      the words are inside, they just don't like the way
my tongue curls colonized—voice continually pulled
back—smoked down when my home smells like safety

*   *   *

inside the AGO, everyone stops
to take photos with Riopelle
glances at
           Morrisseau

and leaves the room

* * *

                    the roots are tangled in my grandmother's hair
                    and sand dune skin—they say tobacco likes to grow
                    where tobacco likes to grow—reaching down deep
                                                   into her silence

                              * * *

in the dream I am four years old
I am standing in the office
with the dead moose
mounted on the wall

I look into his beaded black eyes
and run away

back in the forest, fox is standing still
as sound—the wind rustles—he tilts
his head towards a hole

I know I should follow
but I don't want to go
into that room again

                              * * *

                    sometimes I google dictionaries so the poems
                    can match my dreams—voice continually lulled
                    back— as if now the words think they belong there

the fifth floor said buffalo filled hills with bone
song and Hank Williams Thomas promised
that from the right angle

history is present

still, on the way downstairs a white man
hogs the inner railing

never letting me pass

* * *

I look up fox medicine in the spirit guide
they are all about shapeshifting—learning
to be invisible—moose is all contradictions
feminine energies born with their eyes open

* * *

I want to tell him how my blood beats drum
that I think that is why my grandmother left
that we put so many things in our hearts
we forget
we still have hands

— from *The Malahat Review*

Remember When

Louise Bernice Halfe–Sky Dancer

awasis dreamt she married herself
adorned with full-moon breasts
a phallus and gonads.
When she woke
her body was a full-grown woman
her spirit entwined in a warrior's heart.
She gave birth like any other
bear grunting, groaning, and pushing
forth a blood river of land-filled brawls.
awasis worked like a wolverine
hefty muscles bearing tattoos.
Her feet were the ballet dancer's desire
fingers that traced a cello with the lightness
of a butterfly's wings.
When you see her today
she's the man on stage, her bulge
straining against her ballet tights.
She's the woman wearing workboots
driving a transport loaded with fruit
going cross-country.

Remember when the two-legged
had three, four, five, six, and
sometimes seven: he, she, he-she,
she-he, she-she, and he-he.

In Cree country when people speak
of a man or woman, they refer to them
as he and she. They know that spirit
is neither and is all.

— from *Brick*

River People

Di Brandt

for Tomson & Raymond

I have come now to live with the river people.
I was raised among the earth people, proud
dirt under the fingernails, long rugged silent
days of hoeing and plowing. Electric barbed
wire to keep the cows in, tin granaries bulging
with ripe wheat. Bright orange carrots rooted
improbably, juicy, green feather topped, in
cracked black soil. Meadow larks perched on
the fenceposts along the gravel road,
announcing the morning with their cheery
trilling song.

I lived with the lake people for a while, sand
coloured beaches, blue grey water, sparkling
sky, no fixed borders anywhere. Ground
squirrels darting through the bushes. The
slow *put put put* of the weatherbeaten grey
aluminum boat. Pungent smell of rotted fish,
rustle of dead mayflies, flash of white wings
and sharp beaks. Shots ringing out. Midnight
feast for the whole clan. Too much drink.
Aurora borealis painting the night sky, and
the moon, the moon.

There were the years I lived with the asphalt
and cement people, dedicated to glass and
steel, and cars, and money, and speed.
Pinstriped linen suits over crisp white cuffs,
tooled leather briefcases, colour coded digital
presentations in fashionable Power Point.

Statistics, analyses, tables, maps, reports.
Hurry hurry, faster faster, more more. Belgian
raspberry cider in goldrimmed glasses.
Yachts and sailboats on the canal. Parched
ditches, car accidents, the singing stars
muffled behind inky clouds.

There were the years I lived in the air,
crowded cabins with TV screens built into
the seatbacks, dinners on plastic trays.
Smiling servants everywhere. Lipstick
pantyhose, eye shadow, stilettos. Yellow
turbans and hand embroidered slippers.
Passports, hotel reservations, waitlines,
security checks. Fresh squeezed orange juice
for breakfast, crisp papaya salad for lunch,
piña colada at seven. Ambassadorial
receptions, keynote addresses, interviews.
Pictures in the newspapers.

I have come now to live with the river people.
We sit on the reedy shore and watch the water
flow by, urgently, purposefully, carrying the
continent's pulse and debris firmly along to
the bay we have heard about, on the edge
of a mythical northern ocean, with seal mermaids
and melting ice floes, far away.

We watch the people living on the other side
with their bigger yards and lusher gardens
and louder dinner parties, knowing we live on
the superior wilder, slower, freer side. Don't
we? And they, do they feel pity, or envy,
looking across at us perched on our
unadorned rocks, with our fishing lines and
ragged sprawling nettle and burdock groves?

We chat with the geese. We watch the sun's
reflection as it's going down, a long wavering
red line slashing the water. We sing to the fish.
We scatter many coloured flower petals to the
spirit bones of our beloved remembered drowned,
the overdosed, the lost, the disappeared. The
deep heart's cry of *why, why, why, why, why*. We
pick wild berries, sumach, raspberry, blackberry,
on the shore. The smoke of our tiny backyard
fires, tobacco lit, spirals upward toward the heavens.

My fingers begin to remember how to weave
willow baskets and bright coloured shawls.
My lips begin to mutter the old songs in the old
languages, my tongue curling gingerly around
the strange and familiar sounds. I begin to hear
the babble and gurgle, the *gloog gloog gloog*, at
the earth's deep core. My mind begins to wander
the swirling galaxies. What could I possibly want, more?

— from *Prairie Fire*

Poet Laureate Address, City of Winnipeg
Mayor's Luncheon for the Arts, June 14, 2019
Fort Garry Hotel, Winnipeg, Canada

A Room of My Own

Maureen Scott Harris

My mother had no room of her own
except the one inside her. In it she stored
what she chose not to talk about. No revelations
escaped from it, no family stories fell
from shelves to be burnished or embellished.
She kept herself to herself, a private life
in a private room, door firmly shut when I knocked.

When I was twelve or fourteen, uncertain
where I belonged, I asked if we could see
the family tree her brother was rumoured to have.
We were in the kitchen—was she baking?—
putting pincurls in my hair? *I don't want to know
about the sheep thieves* she said. I remember
she brooked no argument when angered.
Her sayings were rebukes—*if you can't say
something nice, don't say anything at all . . . curiosity
killed the cat . . . you made your bed, now lie in it . . .*
lessons that still can close my throat.

I learned refusal, distanced myself
from family conversation, plunged into books,
chose silence over speech. Here I am
some sixty years later, feeling I betray her
as I write.

       Yet I also have that room in me.
It serves to keep me safe.
It serves to keep people out.

— from *The New Quarterly*

Salutations from the Storm

John Elizabeth Stintzi

Sometimes I wonder
if I'm really the best
person for this body.

"Sometimes" means
daily. "Body" means
cage. "Person" means

nothing at all, unless
you count this ghost, or
this storm. You can see

my haunt in the tired
eyes. In the limbs struck
like exploding oaks

as you assume you know
what this body holds—
which is never me

which may never be me.

I'd like to see my body
with someone else in it.
I just want to see it happy.

— from *The Fiddlehead*

82

the science of holding on

Natalie Lim

Newsweek tells me that time travel
might be possible if we can first locate
an object with infinite density. I don't pretend
to understand why, but Google "infinite density"
anyway, learn how the laws of physics refuse to comply
in certain places, like black holes, like old memories—

could something like that live here?

see the astronauts towing it home on a string,
their padded hands placing it gently on a pedestal
to be feared and admired,
used for the greater good.

we might go to look at it on a Friday night,
pay an entrance fee to watch the scientists
make history obsolete as they shout to be heard
over the mechanical drone of their progress.
we've done it, they'd say,
their faces beaming through bulletproof glass,
and now we will see the future.

the next morning, my local paper will report
the most impressive scientific breakthrough
of the 21st century. I will flip past to the weather

as I reach for a cup of coffee, reach again
to hang a weight on these hands.
anything to slow the ticking,
keep the nectarines unripe, uneaten,
not soft enough yet
to bruise.

I am selfish, see?
everyone I love is now.

I text, pray, hug, call,
check the clock to make sure.
still here.
still here.
still here.

— from *Maisonneuve*

Selkirk, Manitoba

Brandi Bird

There is a storm of wild roses
over Selkirk, Manitoba. They grow
from all sides, stems crooked, blooms
thick over streets: Main, Eveline
and Mercy. The flowers bleed
a soft light like a wound under
water, the Red River a current
growing darker as petals fall
from the sky. They float upstream
to the catfish grounds, to the Interlake,
to the floodway. A scour of petals
on the riverbank, clay pinking
in waves. The lift bridge opens
in the chip of thorns and unfolds
a trellis to drift through, cradling
rosehips on the rusted spokes. The old
water tower disappears from view,
unnames Selkirk; gone in a rush
of green. People turn into stamen
and pistil, merge, become
roses. They grow in the cracks
of streets planted where they stand
pointing at thorns that cut
through the roofs of low-income
housing. Red round berries fall
to the ground, ferment, and the prairie
swallows them drunk and whole. The body
of the town a rose bush, a dry thicket,
a target for lightning strikes,
waiting to catch fire and begin again.

— from *PRISM international*

Shame: a love letter.

Ivan Coyote

Do you remember all of your shame like I do? Does it creep into your chest when you wake up too early? Does it lie there, coiled beneath your scars?

Does it trickle down between the muscles of your back when you sweat inside the shirt you can't make yourself take off, even on the beach on your birthday? Born in August.

We walked along the powdery sand to find a place to put our towels, and I couldn't find any words to explain why I was crying on such a sunny day. Seven days later I can now say out loud that undressing in a crowd reveals what feels like a fading target on my chest, white semi circles where breast is now chest and round pink nipples I have not been able to feel for five years. No one is staring at you, I tell myself. There are all kinds of bodies here, I tell myself. But still. None that look like mine.

What did shame ever teach me, except to be ashamed?

— from *subTerrain*

a simple instruction

Tara McGowan-Ross

"cut towards the darkness in the forest"

> — Crooked Nose, Mountain Man
>   (foreman, [redacted] Contracting, spring 2018)

cut towards the darkness   in the forest, there:
see where the land gives out? where the old-field pines
encroach?[1] cut towards the end   , high
flag (in blue)   so we know where to follow   if we lose
you   .   plant left, which is   right
swing back over the middle ground you   crossed
& allow yourself to be persuaded to where your ancestors
stood, then   further,   looking
ending up   at [   ].   I've cut you
a red line there   by the second-highest tree
on the last line the beetles got.   you'll know the tree
by the way the tree knows you   cut up from [   ]
towards the snowy peak that looks the   proudest
                                             most sorrowful

it's three hundred trees up & then you'll have to cut
        back   towards the darkness
you left behind.   if you get to what [   ] did to
[   ], you've gone too far   don't worry
    about crossing your neighbour's line, name it *forgiveness*.
[or *tomorrow*].   you'll never reach it[2]
then, run back, as quickly as you can on uneven ground
move with *urgency*   it'll all be worth it. hear your real

---

[1] Warren, Robert Penn. *All the King's Men.* New York: Time Incorporated, 1946. Print.
[2] Vuong, Ocean. "Someday I'll Love Ocean Vuong." *The New York Times.* May 4, 2015. Web.

name on my tongue after all these years   sorry it took me
so long   I'll never forget again, until
I do.   anyway   there's a radio
under the tarp and a straight shot if you need to run
              remember what you aren't supposed to run from
              remember the radio is broken and always has been

you know what to do, and I trust you.   the darkness
in the forest: go now   run.

— from *PRISM international*

the stopped clock
Amber Dawn

I was costumed in a white tiger striped bodysuit when I found out
I'd been accepted into the graduate creative writing program
at the University of British Columbia. The bodysuit was one size
too small and my labia majora squeezed out from either side
of the gusset whenever I sat down.

I sat with the other sluts, most of whom I loved like stopped clock,
    around
a vinyl-topped card table inside a corrugated steel barn in Huntsville,
    Alabama.
Our hosts brought warm tamales wrapped in tinfoil
and a one-gallon glass jar of homemade moonshine.

From the moonshine I expected what I expect of every spirit
stronger than seventy proof. I expected a methanol spice akin to
    grappa
and I yearned for the zippered mountain road between Sulmona
    and Pacentro
along which I once vomited in the passenger side footwell of an
    Alfa Romeo.

    The Italian word for vomit is *vomito*. Maybe it's nostalgia, but
            vomito sounds
        so cute. Like something you could name a small pet.

Moonshine flint behind my ears.
My cell phone lit with a 604.

The admission secretary's voice high and bright despite
her calling from four thousand plus kilometres away.
She said *I'm so happy for you*

and *your acceptance letter is in the mail*
and *you should apply for a scholarship.*

Did the secretary know my livelihood was pussy tap?
It's likely the entire selections committee knew.
My writing sample rough packed
with poems about men's billfolds. Ass
ass ass cash and allusion: my nascent body
of work.

Our MC, Rose Anna, announced my big news to the audience.
    Their clanging applause
surprised me. It shouldn't have, because a whore that goes to college
    is adorable.
Live-nude-crook to hit-the-books is a narrative string
any fella can feel good about tucking a fiver into.

The woozy decked stage caught my stiletto. The sound of my knees
pounding plywood barely audible against the sonic boom of
    burlesque.
And besides, what's another bruise?
What's a bruise? What's a bruise? What's a blue moon bruise
to do but pull young blood to and fro like the tide? What's a bruise
but a testament to the sharp art of surrendering to time and place?

And how I surrendered to the stage, quit the clamour
of spectator expectancy, the scream pitched ringing in the round.

I bowed down to ageless filth and glitter and leaked fluid, O strip-
    tease stage
O hallowed ground. I prayed to the ghosts of every hustler who's
    turned rock
ballads into rent, grind into gold. Face downed belly rolled until I
    met god
or a staph infection. Same difference.

This is definitely nostalgia talking. Don't let me (and my tilt
towards glorification) fool you.

The truth is I uprighted myself and finished my routine
just like any other night.

The one concrete detail I recall about the mother, who presented me
with her virgin teenage son that night in the barn, was her pearls.

Nacreous
is the adjective that describes the specific lustre of a pearl. Her
pearls
had flawless nacre. Not like the poor flaking strand
passed down to me by my Nonna
and we were in Alabama.

The mother in pearls was interested
in buying sex for her teenage son.

He must become a man before going off to college.
She was certain it was his virginity that hindered him
from the kingdom and the power of predestined manhood.

What she was unsure of
was how much I should
be paid for my labour.

I sometimes wonder (though do not care in the slightest) if pity
was the reason
I was accepted into the creative writing program at the University
of British Columbia. Wild card candidate, long odds.

An anagram for "creative writing" is "tragic interview."

I would have to veer into fantasy to continue this story
about Alabama. There is nothing I remember
about the virgin teenage son.

To write what little appears on this page, I've superimposed the Geek
from the 1984 film *Sixteen Candles* and alternatively Brian
from *The Breakfast Club*. A John Hughes constructed outcast
crying over thwarted masculinity and a tenuous ability
to subjugate teenaged women's bodies.

I grew up with movies that taught me the meek
shall inherit the prom. Or the Geek shall inherit
access to a blackout drunk cheerleader.

But life rarely mimics a Hollywood ending.
Or does it? One sure thing, sex
work isn't going anywhere.

For as long as I can remember I've been afraid
of the pitiful narrations my body has been
inscribed into and now

that I've refashioned this memory into a poem
I choose to show myself praying on that striptease stage.

On my knees praying, *Please*
            I don't want to be
            afraid anymore.
            I'll do anything, please. Ho paura. Paura lasciami.
                    Please. Unafraid. Please.

You (literally you) are reading queer and desperate poetry, and so
        I already love you like a stopped clock, but if you're wondering

whether or not I took that Alabamian mother's money
to fuck her virgin son then you too better

kneel down and pray.

The other sluts dropped me, and my bag
full of animal-print lingerie and the small grimy bills I earned
in the South, at O'Hare Airport in Chicago. They kept touring
the Midwest: Milwaukee, maybe Minneapolis and eventually
into the lonesome sphere of memory. (These days, if I can't find
an old friend through Google I assume they are dead.)

I flew back to Vancouver to attend the University
of British Columbia, where more than one professor warned me
not to confuse creative writing with therapy.

— from *Arc Poetry Magazine*

Stutters

Roger Nash

For stutterers, Newton got it all wrong.
Unsupported words don't fall
into silence, they just hold their place
and keep trying to, trying to, f-f-fall.

It's reit-it-eration that holds
the world together. Nothing happens
once only: Black Death,
Resurrection, Big Bang, Utopia,

a dog stealing strings of sausages,
that old lady at the door selling
eggs (and her chickens keep laying,
keep laying—cracked eggs).

For a stutterer, easier to speak clearly
in a strange language you're learning to pronounce.
"Sait on jamais." The waitress blows you
a kiss, but you've no idea what you ordered.

In mid-stammer, furniture in a room
moves about unfamiliarly. The sofa's gone missing,
pictures askew on the wall, but the wall,
tight-lipped, still uprightly there.

With the Industrial Revolution, machine-guns
mechanized the reloadable stutter perfectly.
You don't have to aim to mow down the cavalry,
scatter epaulettes of eloquence into the mud.

The tide comes in while you're still trying
to say it's gone out. Sandcastles

wash away, but the girl next to you shucks off
both her blue conversation and red towel.

Eloquently nude enough for both of you.

— from *Prairie Fire*

Thin-Skinned

Susan Haldane

In paradise the suburb is breaking
open, steam abrading lawns
and driveways. News photos show ooze
bubbling from the wound, blackening.
Elsewhere sinkholes rupture
like boils.
                    They used to call me
that too—thin-skinned. Whatsa matter,
Earth, can't take a joke? So many tears
in your parchment skin. Couldn't
I sit you down on a kitchen chair
and fetch the Band-Aids from the mirrored
medicine cabinet? Can't I
kiss it better?

    — from *Grain*

3:00 a.m.

Tim Bowling

Night's middle. Mind's stuck.
Python swallow. Trying to put
a face to the name of a
truth. One cloud
dissolved by another
a passenger train passing
through twilight to dark
Christ losing consciousness
on the cross.
I get up and go out.
Read the front page of the moon
until the print comes off
on my hands. Coyote's breath
the colour of the ribs
almost sticking through its fur.
I hear each pant break
like river ice.
Back in bed, on my back,
I set the tongue's trap
for thought, want
to kill what makes the hour
tick. Can't. Listen
as the panther's paws
erase the pawprints of the cage
of the elevator that rises
before the unpaid admission
and amusement of the mortal laws.

— from *The Malahat Review*

Three for One

Margaret Christakos

Where birds sleep is mysterious. They all
text you at 2 a.m. saying I'm crashing
at Solomon's. Katie's. Nick's. But you
never know for sure. You sit up till
4 a.m. your red pen doodling in the margins
of the Safeway flyer. Numerous bird parts are on
sale. Saturday morning gatecrasher, 3 for 1.
Boneless, skinless. Free range. You note birth and
death dates of all the cousins, how much
you e-transferred yesterday on Utilities. Chisel
birthday lists: Why not plan ahead. Toys R Us's
shuttering its gym-sized outlets. Go online. Used to
be easy. Order medieval executioner, half-turtle
swashbuckler, lamp shade tie-dye kit. Sip
cold mint tea. Sort which one is Solomon. What
corner. Katie who. West or east end
Nick. Do birds
sleep inside tree trunks? Ball up under
leaf clusters? Tremble in a flock of dark
fist shapes on the softball field? Frozen giblets.
Stilled
hearts. Your red nib circles all the
times *FRESH* is set in italic capitals. Why
doesn't anyone have a clue about where
the birds flop? It's minus 22. From
midnight to 5 a.m. they could be stashed
anywhere. Anywhere—Anywhere
at all.

— from *The Malahat Review*

To Whyt/Anthology/Editors

Andrea Thompson

for Sonia Sanchez

Bloom n' Norton
don't collect me no
                        scribblin' by blk women
they ain't rt bout nothin'   !

Don't tell me 'bout
y'r crab bucket philosophy
                        /her 40 yrs of
                        Sound 'n fury   Signifying
(can't see the forest)
                                                    Monkey
jibberish.

                        Blues/jazz/soul po'tree
                        /grows
thick 'n dark down here in the jungle   /bark
like words you can chew through

tastes
like a noose   /unbound
/not forgotten.

Put down that axe, you ain't
got no bizness messin' with these
                        roots'n branches
with the apple of our I

                        /her seeds
                                        all our new beginning

you   dig?

    — from *Arc Poetry Magazine*

12 Rules for Gatekeeping

Kyle Flemmer

1) Amplify disparate peoples and visions,
   decentre ego always.
2) Empower others to make decisions,
   less work for you ;)
3) Make revolving doors of authority,
   get in, then *get out the way!*
4) Chiding "philistines" is police work,
   lead a cheer instead.
5) Twitter is a blessing and a curse,
   and yes, all tweets are poems.
6) Well, not everything is a poem,
   nor should it be.
7) Art is political when activated,
   but dies when disengaged.
8) Sweeping statements are usually wrong,
   about art especially.
9) Avant-garde is a state of mind,
   not a group or style.
10) Distrust apparently cohesive systems,
    live in contradiction.
11) Saying "no" is oftentimes necessary,
    make it tender and decisive.
12) Don't make collaborators regret it,
    this is for them, after all.

— from *filling Station*

Waves

Jana Prikryl

The wind reeled up Broadway kicking a plastic bag
as high as the window cleaners at 57th Street, bringing hands
to lapels as hairdos slapped sideways and up.

Sunlight hit the wind,
wind fell through the light,
and everybody all of a sudden fought to hold a disassembling
    trapeze.

That night the wind remade itself
and shot down Third Avenue, now a black wind, clearheaded,
soaked with dark water repeatedly and repeatedly wrung out.

To walk up the street was to be rinsed,
to lean into the current and hear
its drowned voices, hear the one voice just stating the obvious.

— from *The Walrus*

Weight

Erin Soros

1

Gyms are play rooms and torture chambers and
churches; they smell of rank sweat and Ban and chalk;
they are solitude and intimacy; they are where we go
to think and not to think, to feel and not to feel.
In these sunken retreats I don't run or cycle, don't
take yoga classes or dance the Zumba. I lift weights.
I pick up that base purity and let it greet the air.
I walk to where the weights wait, dark creatures,
humble geometry until we press each shape high.
I know men because I know their jerky movements
and their staccato talk and the instant of tenderness
when they give each other a spot—need a spot?
one will ask, standing in place to offer help before
the response is given. They trust another's hands
with a twenty kilo bar holding another one-hundred
that could slip and clatter through the air to smash
their teeth or their nose or their brain. I remember
a winter morning when the few men who freckled
the gym stopped their lifts, metal gone quiet, and
they stood still to listen to Adele. One day I'll find
someone like you, her lipstick longing floating over
their stink, and I could almost feel the loves and
losses daydreaming across that long mirrored room,
and then the men turned back, a bit more slowly,
somnambulistic and loyal to the familiar repetitive
solidity of weight plates and horizontal bars, relief
of quads and lats, hours carved into arms, each of
their bodies doubled in the reflection as if to prevent
absence. In the weight-cluttered corners of some gyms
I am the only woman, or one more will be like me,

doing pull-ups with weight attached by a leather belt
around her waist, the plate swaying from a chain
between her legs like the largest heaviest cock. We
don't talk, this woman and I, but we'll nod at each
other or sometimes give a thumbs up when one of us
executes an Olympic clean and jerk. And we walk
differently than we would if we walked on pavement
wearing shiny hard-soled shoes—I know that inside
a gym there is a buoyant strength even to my gait,
a comfort within my body, arms and legs swinging
and exposed and yet protected by ropes of muscle,
no man shouting at me or leering at me, not here
when I can look him back in the eye and will do so
every Monday and Wednesday and Friday of this
week and he can count on the next. I have lifted
weights in a seedy basement gym near Hastings
where strong men injected steroids and climbed
on top of each other when doing calf raises, bulky
body over bulky body like two copulating bugs.
"Come on faggot, come on you faggot." I have
lifted weights in a Harlem gym with a blood
red floor within a sprawling complex raised
by the city in exchange for something I can't
remember that the neighborhood didn't want—
sewage treatment or a garbage dump—and that
wouldn't have been built near whites. Men
in this gym wore durags and black t-shirts that
smelled of soap and they were so warm to my
entrance into their lair that each encounter felt
like being welcomed at a party, how they'd open
their arms to show me a free squat rack as if
it was their gift to offer. I once announced to
one of them how much I appreciated that they
never hit on me or harassed me and he responded
harass you? We are *afraid* of you. I worried
he meant that my whiteness frightened him,

this pale ticket that put him at risk even here in
his humid territory, until he pointed out that
pound-for-pound my wiry build pressed more
damned weight than he could. Every day
you come in here like you are going to kick
my ass, the man next to him joined in to tease,
back off, sister, back off. I have lifted weights
in an unairconditioned gym under a steel roof
in an unusually sweltering UK summer, heavy
metal music blasting in a medieval village, men
carrying what is too heavy for their swaying backs
except for that one man, bald and muscly as Mr.
Clean. He had trained as a fitness instructor in
prison and moved with us only on day leave,
returning each night to sleep on a cot in a cell.
He told me he always looked out of windows,
even when he was outside prison and with his
girlfriend he would keep away from the openness
of the green lawn and the reaching street and
would instead sit inside her kitchen, inside that
limit, and gaze out of the glass, constrained but
hopeful, windows show you where freedom is,
he told me. On September 11th in New York City,
2001, when smoke ghosted the avenues, I called
hospitals to see if anyone needed my blood and
no one needed my blood or anything else my
body could give so I walked useless to Columbia
University which was closed but the fitness centre
was open so I descended to the basement gym with
the cobalt blue floor—our blue womb, a professor
of postcolonial literature used to call it—where the
security guards and the doormen and the janitors
had gathered together with the students and the
profs, and we seemed relieved and surprised and
yet not surprised to find each other, here, each one
of us wearing buds tucked into the pockets of our ears

so we could listen to music that promised a journey
far away or listen to news that circled around towers
we couldn't see and yet couldn't escape. We'd rack
a pair of dumbbells we had managed to lift above
our shoulders, struggling again and again, our own
towers that rose and fell and rose and fell. We'd catch
another's eyes, smiling just slightly beyond a horizon
as if even our mouths were lifting weight, because today
we all knew each other's ritual and comfort and shame.

2

I started lifting weight the summer my friend
overdosed on heroin. I wasn't at the party.
When the party ended they came across him
lying on the porch, dawn touching his skin, his
lungs empty, his body stiff and blue and not
waiting, not anymore. He used on weekends,
and I knew it, or should have, from the way
he reminded me of my brother. My brother's
heart had stopped in winter, in his boyhood
bedroom, that still small bed. It was years ago.
It was my father who heard him choking and
ran to his side then to the phone. He couldn't
tell the ambulance the address of the home he'd
lived in twenty years, all the years of his son,
the numbers disappearing from his mind the way
lightning makes everything too visible and too
sharp. Paramedics carried my brother outside,
past my parents who had to wait on the couch.
They shouted at my parents to get out of the way.
He was dead in the moment when his body passed
my mother and father's wake on the couch and then
his body reached the night air and he was tucked into
the ambulance and the paramedics pressed and they
pressed, red flashing, heart quickening. One beat.

The next. My brother returning live like our private
Jesus. Awake in a white box solid as a matchbox car.
His tracks led nowhere. He'd lost four years to a daily
habit. My friend lost the remaining years of his life.
I punched my trainer. He held up those padded black
mitts and I'd whack him fast and mean. Nothing
felt as good. Next to him, a bag's dead weight. Back
and forth hitting, from the bag to the man. I knew
the hunger of the fix. I knew the hunger of hunger.
The summer my friend died of a heroin overdose
I finally visited a doctor who examined the women
who starved themselves, as I had done, narrowing
my adolescence until I became a human needle, one
of those stretched metal statues that are beautiful
because they are not alive. What stomach like a line
could hold need? And on those spindly stiff legs
who could walk or run or dance? A needle is both
the tool that penetrates and a hollow vessel to be
filled. I was such a hungry girl. I walked on soles
unfleshed, the concrete hard and harsh. I rubbed
shoulder bones into sheets, skin raw as my skeleton
tried to escape. I became hard. I knew no one
would hit this body because this body would hurt
no one as much as it did me. When my age doubled
I lifted weight not to gain muscle but to gain bone.
Thirty-three that summer when I rode the elevator
to the doctor of thin women. He told me I had the
bones of an eighty-year old. Osteoporosis sounds
just like what it is. He offered a lifetime of white pills.
The fix, I read alone at the screen, was weight-bearing
exercise. I found my Scottish trainer, trading lessons
on how to write for lessons on how to lift. The plural
possessive, for example, was a good hour's work. We
laughed. We listened to Belle and Sebastian. I fought
in a war and I left my friends behind me to go looking
for the enemy, and it wasn't very long before I would
stand with another boy in front of me. Starvation

lurked at the edges of the gym. Those mirrors showed
that girl. Boy girl; pencil sketch; lead tip tears the page.
At age sixteen she'd reached my adult height at half
my adult weight. I am my body doubled. I could fit
one of me inside. A skeleton in the closet, so many
years away I will never not see my flesh emaciated,
internal shadow, that body under this body, child
sight to draw the eye and repulse it. Women stared
and talked about me all through those starving hours
of my sixteenth year just as the teenagers did at school,
as if I couldn't hear them, as if my eyes were already
dead. Look. She's frightening. Disgusting. My friend
is dead. I hit the black mitts hard and long as I could.
I'm going to give you the biggest hug, my trainer said.
When we finish, I'm going to give you the biggest biggest
hug. He taught me the big difference between free
weights and machines was that weights mimic the shift
of natural movements, the way your own body has to
support your balance in real life. Machines, he said,
give you too much help. I pulled metal sleds up and
down an empty road. Go! We masked our affection
with the wounding cruelty of insults. He called me
Skinny Malinky and Spider Man and Olive Oyl. I said
he reminded me of Shrek. And with your round bald
head, every day when I look at my roll-on deodorant
I can't help but think of you. By the end of the summer
I had gained fifteen pounds. All my curves, I said full
of pride as I flexed arms to beat my father's, are in
my biceps. I could bench press the weight of a man.
My friend used to enter his Subaru through the hatch-
back because none of the doors worked. The last time
I saw him he was crawling into the bowels of a car. Now
I saw him when he wasn't there—was that him, playing
basketball with a group of kids? Was that him, dread-
locks swaying over a suit? It never was. Never would be.
My brother OD'd just days before Christmas and my father
told us on Christmas, after my sister and I opened our gifts,

and I ate dinner, because my parents didn't want to ruin it.
Derek OD'd on heroin, my father told us, he died on Thursday,
we have to go visit him in the detox. I stuck on that second
clause and couldn't reach the third. Time hung suspended
like one last breath. We reached the detox and he was alive
under a curtain of red and green chains, the construction
paper twisted and taped, and he was hallucinating that
my father was beating him. My father looked away, clenched
his coffee cold, tearing pieces from Styrofoam. My brother
scratched his raw face, his bruised arms as thin as mine
once had been, as my chest now remained, as if he had
become the daughter while I, breastless, had become my
father's son. My trainer put the plates on the bar for me,
and when I had finished lifting them he took them away
and reracked them, knowing each time what my body
could lift and what it could not, these gentle calculations,
all my effort laced by his hands. I carried groceries, bags
and bags full, everything suddenly easier than it had been
before. Protein shakes and salmon, apples, eggs and rice.
You have to feed the muscle, my trainer told me. Carbs
before you lift, carbs and protein after. Care in all these
calories that enabled my arms to press the weight high
enough for him to say you did it, lass. For his birthday
I bought a Shrek chia pet that invoked his balding dome,
how the hair sprouted tentative but optimistic. My father
and I tossed ropes over the wire fence that barricaded
the gym, criss-crossing the ropes under the blackening sky,
suspending the wrapped chia pet bobbing in the middle
of that tensile web as if my present had no weight at all.

3

My one review on RateMyProfessors.com says Professor
Soros can squat a ton of weight. I lived for a year in a
college town, pressed iron at a college gym, the kind

full of frat boys and sorority girls, that offers free towel
service and TVs attached to every treadmill. I'd lunge
across the length of the floor, my legs opening and closing
like scissors, my eyes forward, as if I had the place to myself.
One of my students told me that when I did my pull-ups
people stopped what they were doing to look. Why? She
laughed. Your muscles ripple, she said. At night I tucked
myself into a small space, attic apartment where I found
a photograph of the landlady's daughter—she looked
happy, a teenager sunlit in one of those awkward A-frame
dresses squeezed full of bridesmaid. She'd have reached
my age. Exactly. That long fall she died from her devotion
to starve herself. I spoke to the landlady the day she heard.
She wanted to know if I had a car. Do you need to park
your car? I told her I did not have a car. If you need to
park your car, she said, you have to be careful not to
block me. I need to be able to get out, she said. The odd
angles of her urgency reminded me of what happened
to language the afternoon I called the secretary of the art
history department to ask about my friend. He and I
used to meet every Wednesday evening to hover in
each other's company while we discussed hard books—
we were trying to understand Lacan's Real; we both
possessed that kind of desperate sincerity, small talk
dense as an atom. Then my friend suddenly stopped
coming. I hadn't heard his voice for days and now his
phone had been disconnected, just a weird woman's
robot syllables saying this cold line. I wasn't in touch
with his other friends, the partying crowd. Do you
know where he has gone? He died, the secretary said,
and the sounds thudded in the phone, the sounds
dropped to the floor, thing word, word thing, mirror
consonants, *d d d d* beginning and *d d d d* end. It
was an echo I could not stop. The landlady's daughter
had once slept in the bed that was now mine, her heart
starving. In the morning I'd walk to the college gym

and lift weight. I gripped that plainness, that constancy,
that repetition. When I was a teenager I stopped eating
because it was the only way I knew how to disappear.
I would be no woman. Not for me my mother's gift
for tender food. I walked the highway in the August
heat in my father's down coat and still my body shivered.
In the time before this shook me something else did.
I was stalked by a boy who shot himself. I can say it now,
this tidy sentence, myself the subject of the passive
voice, the boy an object; each time I break the wrapper
on these sounds, I find the words get a little bit lighter
when they shouldn't be this light. His name the same
as my brother's, my familiar strange, as if he took love
and broke it. I clasped the cord. I'm in the backyard,
he used to threaten over the telephone. I'm watching
you. I'm going to get you. It's going to happen. I
never knew when it would. In the college gym a man
had begun to stand behind me, no weight in his grip.
Sometimes he'd reach up and touch a metal bar, just
tapping it, as if he were checking its place or making
sure it was there. I'd move to another part of the gym
and he'd walk behind me, and there I could feel he was
looking at me, the way my student said people were
looking. My leg was broken, but I hobbled to cables,
determined at least to keep the strength in my arms.
I had read if you build one leg it will build the other,
a circuitry of messages sent through flesh and bone,
sibling limbs, one taking the weight two should brace.
I was good on a pair of crutches. I could do tricks.
Students at the gym gave me advice and high fives.
You should tell people you fell doing stunts off a roof.
I couldn't tell people how easily thinness can break.
Bone memory, fibula snapping clean when I flailed on
 ice, muscle a spasm around my calcium fragility to
protect it. He came closer, patting me, crutches his
permission. He sent emails. Left gifts on my doorstep.

A backscratcher he'd carved for those sensitive parts
that are hard to reach. Just before closing, the gym
already dark, I'd find him in the changing room. Are
you decent? Are you decent? Oh but you are never
decent! I grasped my shirt, a barrier. He'd leer, sway,
say he was there to collect towels, which I knew was
not his job. My armpits ached from the effort to hold
myself up. Do you have enough towels? He'd ask me
standing outside the shower, just on that side of the
curtain. He laughed when he frightened someone he
hadn't met, a Black woman. But I thought it was you
showering! I raged at him in her defence, this woman
I was not. One night, a gift, inside my locker inside
the women's changing room, that intimate space inside
an intimate space. He had access to the code. He knew
his way in. When I was in high school, the boy who stalked
me had pried loose my locker to rip apart my notebooks,
paper white as chicken feathers inside the metal walls
graffitied with his initial in red paint, *D* distorted and
dripping like it had been killed. *DDDD*. Now in this
college town I opened my locker to discover it already
opened. Chance rhyme shot my heart, dread pulsing
my body the way it quivers a mouse. If this was a
movie I would insert a commercial break. A car would
glide down a road, some grace of vehicular ballet, no
traffic, dashboard laid out before the driver's fingers
like the body of a lover. Then another commercial, soft-
lit, some insurance, security, a husband and a wife. You
would return to see me talking with a Vancouver doctor
about a sexual harassment case, cumbersome term that
didn't fit the gestures in that gym, legalese the school
made mine when they asked me to come forward to
lodge a complaint. In the movie you first see mountains
and then the camera spans a crowded beach; you know
you are in Vancouver, in a hot wide open summer far
from that town. I am safe here, or should be, having flown

back to be with my family before testifying in the civil case.
In the stern tone of medical professionals the doctor says
she wants to put a heart monitor on me, a strap wrapped
around my nipples like some permanent hug. Your heart,
she says, it thinks someone has a gun to your head. His
or mine, I said, it doesn't matter which. Someone could
fall. Someone could just stop taking it all. But I don't
show up to be equipped with this tool sensitive enough
to read my heart. I begin the search for my wedding,
which I should find in the store where my sister worked.
The store is called Liberty. Do you know the way to liberty?
Turn left, someone says, and I think I have been left, all
the people who leave me, all the places I have departed.
Now how to find my loved ones waiting at the wedding?
Billboards give me some clues. The alphabet ricochets and
cracks. Signs on the sidewalk and the cell phone riff raff
rift left lift life lie like let me in please leave the premise a
poem as glass doors shut shatter letter leaves bounce on
concrete. You are blocking. I was in the present tense
and the past tense at the same time. I wore gym clothes
because I was on the way to the gym, or from the gym, or
at the gym, the entire city of Vancouver was a gym and
the man who stood behind me and tapped weights was
here, on the street, brown eyes leering within the faces of
strangers. A hallucination is as flimsy and translucent as a
Kleenex. Toss one dream and grab another. My brother
on the streets approached people he didn't know to say
he was opening at BC Place. A musician, he told them, I'm a
rock star, heroin injecting this longing with possible shape.
He offered his signature; a few people accepted his looping
D, inked evidence that he was once there. He went back
to his child bed and his last dose. Breath stopped. Breath
started in the ambulance as if breath is not inside the body
but outside it, and can be reached only by leaving home. I
visited him in the detox and I visited him in the treatment

centre, watching the hush in his glance. The first person
to visit the psych ward was my fitness trainer. He lied
to the staff, declared himself family. He brought me *Okay*
magazine. He eyed the crazies, called me crazy, said
he always knew. You look good in mint blue. This
place is *One Flew Over the Cuckoo's Nest*, any time
you want to get mad at the staff just think the word
lobotomy. Look at all this great material. You're a
writer. Try to stay here longer. I'm a writer? Words
floated around us. Or words were water and we were
the ones floating. Why'd you bring cake? You know
I don't like sweets. It's a nutcake, he said. His grin. That
I grasped his levity made me feel I'd be okay. In the meager
yard of the hospital I led the patients through a series of
exercises, each of us pretending to hold weights in hand.
The catatonic man did a snake dance, thin arms twirling
above his head. I stood momentarily sure, telling everyone
to squat. In the days that followed—pills and ill rituals,
our drooling, complaining when someone changed the TV,
shuffled walk with our plastic dining trays—the drugs began
to root, until my body became weight itself, sullen and still.

4

Sometimes when you are lifting especially heavy you
will push for that fourth or fifth rep and falter, muscle
twitching, weight wobbling at the half-way point or
even just a few inches from where it began. You hold
it, limbo game, and then it sinks back into your body.
Someone is waiting, face above yours, upside down
mouth and nose and eyes, palms outstretched, and they
are saying with all the confidence they don't themselves
need, not for this exercise which is only yours in this
moment: one more, you got this, you can do it. And you

cannot. Or no one is there: you lift alone, danger
you know, solitude you prize, and you are trapped
underneath this weight we all call free. Weight
on your chest, weight on your breath, like it could
kill you, the weight of a stone once used to murder
witches and the men who cavorted with them. I am
more careful now. I wait until the afternoon, when
the clinging antipsychotic fog begins to lift, and the
gym is crowded, here in Toronto where I have arrived,
glass home on a corner: the JCC where movies play and
women often equal the men. Hanukah decorations line
the front desk, tiny candles for sale to benefit children.
You need your identity card to enter the door, white
rectangle swiped across the black reading machine
releasing a high beep and a red flash to let you know
you belong, the security guard nodding as you cross
the threshold to let you know no one can enter who
does not. In this gym I yawn and the men tell me to
go home and have a nap. I will never tell them how
I fight the dragging effects of the pills, pink pills, blue
pills, soft colours that match my workout clothes as if
everything in my life should rhyme. My muscles
weaken as I swallow. And still I return to the push
and the pull. Toddlers linked hand-to-hand waddle
bright on the way to the tumbler room. I wanted
to have a baby and I did not. I never got to carry a
bulbous weight at the centre of my flesh, watery
future, six or seven pounds, the kind of weight that
women's hands caress. Unmarried I then wanted to
adopt, risked scrolling their faces as if I could choose,
but who would place a child in the arms of a woman
who holds so many pills? Windows in this gym are high
on white plaster walls, slits narrow as half-closed eyes,
the gym sunk below ground so all we can see are legs
as crowds hurry past so it reminds me of the basement

apartment of *Laverne and Shirley*. 1, 2, 3, 4, 5, 6, 7, 8
Schlemiel! Schlimazel! Hasenpfeffer Incorporated!
We count our metal hopscotch, our reps and our sets.
I am clumsy now. An old woman with white hair
smiles at me as she yanks the tricep bar to where
her breasts used to be. The ceiling ducts are grey
with insulation. Hoar frost, cat fuzz, the sleep
in the corners of my eyes. The rows of fluorescent
lights cast us in a mauve otherworldly glow. I do
my best. I lunge and yawn. I squat and yawn. On
days when I am scared to face a blank screen with
my tired mind, I still walk to this gym and return to
the familiar heft and heave. In between lifts I scratch
thoughts on scraps of paper or on a Kleenex I nudge
into my sports bra, the pen breaking the delicate
tissue. On my satisfied way home I talk to one of
the men bumming for coins outside the Metro and
he tells me he used to lift weights: meat, he says,
I worked in a meat plant, cows and pigs, I lifted a
hundred-thousand pounds a day. A hundred-
thousand? A hundred-thousand, he says. That
was before the accident, he says, his eyes like a
cloud shielding the sun. Now I'm on a pension, you
know, so I only do this a few days a week. He points
to the ground where he sits next to a plastic cup half-
full of change. Push to failure, I tell my students,
you break the muscle to repair it. You write as hard
as you can and then let it rest. I don't know they grasp
the metaphor, the persistent perspiration required
to take something to the limit, the day of nothing when
you wait for the promise of molecular healing, and the
reliance on others as the weight threatens again to fall.
You work and you wait for the time it wavers, it sinks,
yet you hold it in place, muscle flailing, and this time you
push the weight, your chest's lover that wants to touch

down, you breathe, you breathe again, you raise it higher,
and then higher, with the relish of a man lifting his child
over his shoulders, keeping the metal bar as steady as
a beam tugged up a skyscraper's skeletal new frame.

— from *The Malahat Review*

CONTRIBUTORS' COMMENTARY AND BIOGRAPHIES

Kazim Ali was born in the United Kingdom to Indian parents. His family migrated to Canada in the early 1970s and he was raised on Treaty 1 (Winnipeg) and Treaty 5 (Jenpeg) land. He currently lives on traditional Kumeyaay land in San Diego, California, where he teaches at the University of California. The author of many books of poetry, fiction, and essays, his forthcoming books include the collection of poetry *The Voice of Sheila Chandra*, and a nonfiction book about the Jenpeg Generating Station and the Pimicikamak First Nation of Northern Manitoba entitled *Northern Light: Power, Land, and the Memory of Water*, both available from Goose Lane Editions.

Of "Origin Story," Ali writes, "I am often asked the question 'where are you from?' and like many transnational people, especially people from postcolonial backgrounds, it is a complicated question to answer. I was born in one place, have cultural ties to another, and was raised in a third, a fourth, a fifth. My parents, like many migrants, moved for a host of reasons—economic, political, social. No question has an easy answer. I tried to answer this question many different ways and in many different genres. This poem is one approach to it, my new nonfiction book *Northern Light* is yet another. The idea of a country as a national project—a cultural and social experiment called 'Canada' or called 'the United States of America' or even 'India' depends on a lot of fictions, fictions that must be commonly accepted by the people inside those cartographically delineated national borders. But a person is not what can be documented, a community is not one that can be legislated into borders."

Amber Dawn is a writer and educator living on unceded territories of the Musqueam, Squamish and Tsleil-Waututh First Nations (Vancouver, Canada). Her debut novel *Sub Rosa* (2010) won the Lambda Literary Award for Debut Lesbian Fiction and the Writers' Trust of Canada Dayne Ogilvie Prize. Her memoir *How Poetry Saved My Life: A Hustler's Memoir* (2013) won the Vancouver Book Award. Her poetry collection *Where the words end and my body begins* (2015) was a finalist for BC Book Dorothy Livesay Poetry Prize. Her sophomore novel *Sodom Road Exit* (2018) was a finalist for the Lambda Literary Award for Lesbian Fiction, the BC Book Ethel Wilson Fiction Prize, and a Sunburst Award for Excellence in Canadian Literature of the Fantastic She currently teaches creative writing at Douglas College, as well as guest mentors at several drop-in, community-driven spaces in the Downtown Eastside, an area impacted by poverty-related issues and beloved for its tenacity and creativity.

Amber Dawn writes, "The stopped clock is used in simile twice in the poem: firstly, to describe the narrator's love for a group of sister sex workers; and secondly, when the narrator addresses the reader directly by saying, 'I already love you like a stopped clock.' Stopping the clocks at the time of a loved one's death is a practice used in my Italian Catholic faith—a practice that allows us to mourn for as long as we need without concern for how time is passing outside of the grieving space. 'the stopped clock' is not a poem about death, though. I wrote the poem to mark the occasion of being accepted in a graduate program in creative writing. The poem is a paradoxical celebration. I, a rough queer, experiential sex worker from a poor upbringing, had been welcomed into the most reputable creative writing program in the country, a program that I already understood, at the time, would put me in a fraught relationship with my own personal narrative. Who I was as a storyteller was about to be changed. Through the image of the stopped clock, I attempt to suspend this pivotal moment to both tenderly love and grieve for the guileless woman I was before my graduate work and my professional publishing career began."

Billy-Ray Belcourt is from the Driftpile Cree Nation and lives in Vancouver, where he is an assistant professor in the creative writing program at the University of British Columbia. His books are *This Wound is a World*, *NDN Coping Mechanisms*, and *A History of My Brief Body*.

Belcourt writes, "'Cree Girl Explodes the Necropolis of Ottawa' is a rebuttal to a trend in Indigenous art-making that risks a politics of freedom in the aestheticization of suffering. I wanted to imagine what a liberatory film might be about, how it might refuse to make trauma into an object of curiosity. It is also something of a work of feminist utopian fiction, as I set my sights on a post-Canada future where the protagonist is a Cree girl."

Brandi Bird is a Two-Spirit Saulteaux and Cree poet from Treaty 1 territory currently living and learning on Musqueam, Squamish, and Tsleil-Waututh land in so-called Vancouver. Their poetry has been published or is forthcoming in *Poetry is Dead*, *PRISM international*, *The Puritan*, *The Fiddlehead*, *Brick* and *Room Magazine*. Their chapbook *I Am Still Too Much* was published with Rahila's Ghost Press in Spring 2019

Bird writes, "'Selkirk, Manitoba' is a poem about my hometown and how I escaped it. My memories of growing up there whirl wildly in my brain, unruly and dense, so I made it that way in poetry. The wild roses in the poem are a conflict, like any conflict I had when I was young. The roses manifest and transform the landscape until there's no option left but to burn it down like a farmer's field after harvest. But this isn't a nihilistic burn. I hope, with this poem, that there is room for growth and change in small towns all across the country because, as a queer Indigenous person, growing up in such a place felt like a threat. I often felt like I was the threat. This poem is a response to that feeling."

Selina Boan is a moniyâw (white settler)/nehiyaw poet living on the traditional, unceded territories of the Musqueam, Squamish, and Tsleil-Waututh peoples. Her work has been published widely and she received *Room Magazine*'s 2018 Emerging Writer Award. In 2017, she won the National Magazine Award for Poetry. She works as a poetry editor for Rahila's Ghost Press and is a member of The Growing Room Collective.

Of "Minimal Pairs are Words Holding Hands," Boan writes, "I began writing this poem after learning about minimal pairs in Nêhiyawêwin. Minimal pairs are two words that have only one sound difference. I was curious to play within these word pairings, to see what kinds of connections might arise between them. I also wanted to practice the words, to repeat and remember their sounds and meanings. I chose to include translations for the Nêhiyawêwin words because it mirrored my own learning at that time. Much of this poem reaches towards the challenges, deep reverence, shame, and joy that accompany the process of my (very slow) learning of Nêhiyawêwin. There is an inherent tension and violence between English and Nêhiyawêwin; I am mindful of the complexity of negotiating language learning and my responsibilities as a person of European and Nêhiyaw heritage. How do I challenge the impact and legacy of violent assimilation policies on my own being and the landscapes I inhabit? Nêhiyawêwin was spoken by my nimosôm and nôhkom on my birth father's side. As a result of residential school and other assimilation tactics used by the Canadian government, my birth father can understand Nêhiyawêwin but can only speak a few words. For me, the act of learning Nêhiyawêwin holds grief, frustration, kinship, and connection. This poem jumps around a lot and threads throughout many narratives; there are family histories, parties, heartbreaks, anxiety, love. This poem attempts to build connection through its leaping logic, to hold hands with images and narratives that initially don't feel connected but are."

Margret Bollerup lives in the middle of a cow field at the top of a mountain in Chilliwack, BC. Other little mum-related pieces have appeared in *Maisonneuve, Grain, CV2, The New Quarterly,* and another is forthcoming in *Arc.*

Bollerup writes, "'Dementia and common household objects' is one of the first in a series of poems focused on my mum's long, slow slide into mixed (vascular & Alzheimer's) dementia. She was diagnosed in 2008 while still a practicing physician, and this piece is from a few years after that, when I still found each small cognitive change momentously strange. It seems almost silly, now. Then, things like the circularity of conversations with her seemed so terrifying (*oh no, what does this mean, what is coming next, what awful unknowable thing is happening right in front of me*) that I wasn't able to connect with her, not truly. I couldn't (wouldn't?) hold on to her in those moments, and I wouldn't (couldn't?) write much about what was happening to her, to our family. I feel now like I abandoned her by being so very afraid. I am full up with guilt, but also with gratitude: that I caught this particular moment, that I can show it to you, that I only have to read it to be there again with her, back when she still knew me. A small, heart-shattering/lifting coincidence: the email asking that this piece be included in this anthology arrived on my little mum's birthday this year. *Someone's birthday. Hers.*"

Rita Bouvier is a Métis writer from Saskatchewan. Her third book of poetry, *nakamowin'sa for the seasons* (Thistledown

Press, 2015) was the 2016 Sask Book Awards winner of the Rasmussen, Rasmussen, and Charowsky Aboriginal Peoples' Writing Award. Rita's poetry has appeared in literary anthologies, musicals and television productions, a children's book, and has been translated into Spanish, German, and Cree-Michif of her home community of sakitawak—Île-à-la-Crosse in Treaty 10 territory, the historic trading and meeting grounds of Cree and Dene people.

Bouvier writes, "Who am I? Where do I come from? Who are you? Where do you come from? 'deeper than bone' is a remembering—an outcome of deep listening as observer, participant, and leader for the last thirty years in the World Indigenous Peoples' Council on Education (WIPCE), a movement that holds a space of community and belonging. Within our cultural diversity is oneness we honour upon greeting and meeting one another. Through our languages, we inscribe ourselves on the lands we inhabit on the earth and then honour our ancestors by sharing stories about the diverse knowledge and perspectives we have gained about the great mysteries that we are all a part of. 'deeper than bone' will be part of my next collection—creative interventions borne out of my experience and place in the world that is uncertain and sometimes spiritless. Following the release of my last collection, *nakamowin'sa for the seasons* (2015), Idle No More had erupted and the calls to action by the Truth and Reconciliation Commission into residential schools were front and centre in Canada. On a larger environmental and societal scale, historian and philosopher Yuval Noah Harai, in a CBC Radio interview in 2018, observed that the biggest threats to human beings were climate change, nuclear war, bigotry and convergence of artificial intelligence with biotechnology. But, all of this was before the COVID-19 pandemic."

Tim Bowling lives in Edmonton. Like Thomas Hardy, he believes that a poet touches the hearts of others by exposing his own. A Guggenheim Fellow and six-time finalist for major national prizes in three different genres, he is the author of twenty books of poetry and prose.

Of "3:00 a.m.," Bowling writes, "This is a poem about middle age, about having aging parents and young adult children and worrying about them so that you have a hard time sleeping. I like to create original metaphors and music in my poems, so the python's slow devouring of a meal and Christ's slow death combine with the coyote's breathing and the mind's repetitive thought to (hopefully) form a kind of frantic staccato rhythm that replicates anxiety. But I do also write funny poems sometimes! It's good to employ a broad canvas."

Frances Boyle lives in Ottawa. Her second poetry book is *This White Nest* (Quattro Books, 2019). She is also the author of *Tower*, a novella (Fish Gotta Swim Editions, 2018), *Seeking Shade*, a short story collection (The Porcupine's Quill, 2020), and several chapbooks. Awards for her work include the Diana Brebner Prize, and the Great Canadian Literary Hunt. Frances grew up on the prairies, and maintains strong ties to the west coast. www.francesboyle.com

Boyle writes, "As so very many of my poems do, 'Pegging Out Washing' began with a prompt. This time the challenge (posed by Ottawa poet Michelle Desbarats) was to write about an everyday activity, with seduction as a subtext. I always feel that there is something flirtatious in the way a breeze will nudge and toss clothes until they undulate on the line, so I ramped up the sensuous in drafting what became the second half of the poem. But I wanted a contrast, so I brought in the basement clothesline, as well as the negative aspects of using a clothes dryer, and (for me, the very worst!) those scented dryer sheets. As a result, the indoor and outdoor sections ended up with quite different rhythms and feels. Images and a bit of synesthesia drove the poem, but I tried to use sounds throughout that would evoke the physical, especially touch and scent. Paring down my early drafts to highlight internal rhyme, alliteration and assonance helped improve the flow."

Di Brandt lives in Winnipeg. She has published numerous acclaimed and award-winning poetry collections, including the bestselling *questions i asked my mother*, recently reissued in a thirtieth-anniversary tribute edition, with afterword by Tanis MacDonald; *Agnes in the sky*; *mother, not mother*; *Now You Care*; *Walking to Mojácar*, with French and Spanish translations by Charles Leblanc and Ari Belathar; and most recently, *Glitter & fall: Laozi's Dao De Jing, Trans*inha*lations*. "River People" received the Gold National Magazine Award for 2020.

Of "River People," Brandt writes, "I recently served as the City of Winnipeg's inaugural Poet Laureate, for 2018-2019. I enjoyed the gig very much, and became used to thinking of the city, the place as well as the people, as both the subject and recipient of my poems. This is where I've lived the longest, and I think of Winnipeg as 'home.' But I have lived affectionately in other landscapes as well, both urban and rural, at different times in my life; they have left their mark on me. I was reflecting on 'place' as cultural and land practice rather than location or landscape as such. I was thinking about the way experiences tend to layer one on top of another as we get older. I'm happy for the privilege of having lived long enough for this to begin to happen with me. So this is an 'elder poem,' gathering together the memories of different places I've been lucky enough to live in for awhile, and the vastly different cultural and land practices of each. Canada is such a vast and diverse country! All these different kinds of engagements can happen here, next to each other! The poem is also about aging, about looking beyond the diverse landscapes of this world to the vast other dimensions out there in the multiverse, waiting to be explored in the foreseeable future. How grateful I am for it all!"

Rob Budde teaches creative writing and ecopoetry at the University of Northern British Columbia in Prince George. He has published eight books (poetry, novels, interviews, and short fiction). His most recent books are *declining america* and *Dreamland Theatre* and he currently co-edits *Thimble-berry Magazine: Art + Culture in Northern BC.*

Budde writes, "'Blockade' is a series I started as a response and a contribution to the ongoing political actions in Northern 'British Columbia' having to do with traditional Indigenous land rights and the actions of government and pipelines corporations. In particular, I am a longtime settler supporter of the Unist'ot'en and Wet'suwet'en in their quest for land rights. The text is an attempt to perform a literal & figurative blockade on the page—to interrupt colonial incursion and colonial poetics at the same time. The poem is designed to be painted on plywood and placed across a road or railway."

Mugabi Byenkya has spent the last three years working between Canada and Uganda, spending six months of each year in Toronto. He is an award-winning writer, poet, and occasional rapper. In 2018, Mugabi was featured, by Writivism—East Africa's largest literary festival—as one of fifty-six Ugandan writers who have contributed to Uganda's literary heritage between 1934 and 2018. His debut *Dear Philomena* was named a Ugandan bestseller in the same year. In 2019, Mugabi was named out of hundreds as one of three finalists to be Realwheels Playwright-In-Residence and the recipient of the inaugural Realwheels Encouragement Award.

Byenkya writes, "'If I Die Bury Me Next To My Father' is an homage to the refrain and rhyme pattern 'If I Die/When I Die, Bury me . . .' that I discovered through hip-hop. Rappers from 2Pac to 2 Chainz have used this refrain to meditate on their mortality and to illustrate where they expect their life to come to an end. From 2Pac proselytizing 'Even when I die, they won't worry me / Mama don't cry, bury me a G' to 2 Chainz proudly proclaiming 'If I die, bury me inside the Louis store' and even UGK rapping 'If I die or should I say if I go, bury me in Hiram Clarke next to the Come N Go.' These different refrains are all true to the characters of the rappers they represent which caused me to question my relationship with death and resting places. Where would I be buried if/ when I die? The most likely answer to that question is, right next to my father. Unlike most people, I've always known where I will be buried. My family has been burying loved ones in the family graveyard behind the house my father was raised in since before I was born. I remember picking out my burial plot while playing tag with my little sister in the grave-yard/my late grandparent's backyard. Writing this poem was a way for me to provide my contribution/homage to the hip-hop refrain and a greater meditation on death, white suprem-acy and the terror of living in a police state."

Dell Catherall is a retired teacher-librarian living in Vancou-ver. Her passion for poetry was aroused when she took her first creative writing course at UBC. Her poems have been published in *Arborealis: A Canadian Anthology of Poetry*, the *Federation of BC Writer's Literary Writes, Event* and *The New Quarterly*. She is currently working on a collection of poems about her husband's garden in times of grief, anger, and love, titled *A Garden in the Rain*.

Catherall writes, "I first became interested in sestinas when I read *In Fine Form: The Canadian Book of Form Poetry*. It describes the sestina as a poem consisting of six unrhymed stanzas of six lines each, followed by a three-line envoy, and features an intriguing pattern of word repetitions well suited to writing about obsession. A perfect fit—my hus-band designs his garden for a 33-foot city lot, six raised beds and six levels of deck. The fig tree grows in a large pot placed beside the stone bird bath. We've been obsessed with each other since grade ten. Over time, we've learned to respect and expand boundaries. Navigating marriage and writing a sestina challenge one to find spontaneity within structure. The final words in the first stanza came quickly: I see the world through *purple* framed glasses; we burn candles at din-ner every *eve*; as a child, my husband worked in his mother's *garden*; I have been his *wife* for 50 years; a *fig* is the sexiest fruit imaginable; we celebrate moments of *perfection* every day. How do I use my six words to reflect passion? It took five more years to create 'Fig Sestina.'"

Margaret Christakos is attached to this earth. Hailing from Sudbury, Ontario, she has lived in Toronto since 1987. She has published ten collections of poetry, most recently *charger* (Talonbooks, 2020), a novel, and an intergenre poetic memoir, *Her Paraphernalia: On Motherlines, Sex/Blood/Loss & Selfies* (Bookhug, 2016). In 2017, WLU Press published her selected poems, *Space Between Her Lips. Dear Birch* is forthcoming in 2021 with Palimpsest.

Of "Three for One," Christakos writes, "As a parent of three young adults, I have numerous memories of frightful nights during their teenaged years when their whereabouts were undefined. This poem is part of a series of poems called 'Awoken by the Radio,' written directly upon waking to an 8 a.m. alarm in the depths of winter during my University of Alberta residency in Edmonton in 2018. Most of the poems are prompted by (for the most part, grim) radio news stories and are long and meandering, harder to place in poetry journals; this poem's succinct imagery and second-person perspective reflect the icy logic of parental insomnia."

Ivan Coyote is a writer and storyteller, born and raised in Whitehorse, Yukon, and currently living in Vancouver. They are the author of twelve books, including *Tomboy Survival Guide* (shortlisted for the Hilary Weston Prize for Non-Fiction), and *Rebent Sinner* (nominated for two BC Book Prizes). In 2017 Coyote was given an honorary doctorate from Simon Fraser University, and in 2020 they were the recipient of the Writer's Union of Canada's Freedom to Read Award.

Coyote writes "I wrote 'Shame: a love letter.' longhand, on the back of a utility bill, in the wee hours, after waking up long before dawn from a strange and sweaty nightmare. I had just returned home from spending time in Sweden, with my partner Sarah's family. I'm pretty sure I was the first trans person they had spent any kind of time with, and we were all unsure how to navigate the topic of who I was, I think. I don't speak much Swedish, either, so I often felt very alone and separate from everyone else, even though they are kind and good people. I very much felt like the other. I remember waking to this feeling of shame sitting heavy on my chest, almost a physical weight pinning me down, or like a visitation from a certain kind of ghost I had read about. I just scribbled the words out, trying to capture this impulse of wishing my difference away, because it had become a thing that sat and grew in between me and the people I was attempting to connect with, or at least exist among."

Barry Dempster lives in Holland Landing, Ontario. Twice nominated for the Governor General's Award for Poetry, he is the author of sixteen collections of poetry. He has been a finalist twice for the Ontario Premiers Award for Excellence in the Arts. He was also nominated for the 2014 Trillium Award for his novel, *The Outside World*. His most recent books are the poetry collection *Late Style*, published by Pedlar Press and long-listed for the Raymond Souster Award, and a new volume of short fiction, *Tread & Other Stories*.

Of "From Cocks to Wings," Dempster writes, "Every time spring bursts back on the scene, I find myself taken by surprise, a voice inside me turning mucky and peppered with little green shoots. 'The Daffodil Strut' or 'The Lord is My Lilac'—truth is, I'll sing along to just about anything with a glistening of pollen on it. Standing on tip-toes, sniffing the bottom cherry blossom branches, is one of the few positions I pray in anymore. Most years (come April), I head for New York City's Central Park, where I once outran a gang of young thugs in order to hear Paul Auster give a reading on the West Side. It was dark by the time I reached the street, but the Tavern on the Green was safely resplendent with strings of light. The orchids under the amber ceiling were intoxicating. Wanting to touch them made me human; but actually doing so would have been a trespass, so I drifted into a Barnes & Noble, the garden section, and lost myself in a plethora of shades and colours. I'm with DH Lawrence in cherishing that it's the blood that gives spirit its searing flame. The evening I finally dared the Tavern's menu and ordered a Jayne Mansfield of a bacon burger with a side order of mushrooms as token of my gratitude for keeping the glare of those thugs away, the orchids were soaring into their true brilliance. The bun was soft and the mushrooms made creamy-white nests in the corner of my plate. *Ah, spring!* I sang loud enough for the orchids to be pleased."

Kyle Flemmer is an author, editor, and publisher from Calgary. He is currently undertaking his MA in English Literature at the University of Calgary, where he is researching forms of computer-mediated poetry. He founded The Blasted Tree Publishing Co. in 2014, served as managing editor of *filling Station* magazine from 2018–2020, and has published chapbooks with Simulacrum, above/ground, No Press, and other small presses.

Flemmer writes, "Written during my time as managing editor of *filling Station* magazine, '12 Rules for Gatekeeping' was first presented as an editorial rather than as a poem. My intention was to address persistent feelings of self-consciousness and guilt, as a straight, white male of minor importance, exerting my newfound authority and judgement over the work of diverse and usually far more accomplished writers. That said, editing and publishing are essential to the life cycle of literature, and those people who administrate such endeavours must somehow strike a balance between the contradictory acts of creating space for the use of others and the careful curation of that space. Something of a paradox arises. Always authority implies its own limitation, always rules and lists beg the question of omissions and addendums. Who is being left out and by what right have I positioned myself to make that decision?

How will I know if I've done an adequate job of compensating for my prejudices and blind spots? I don't have the answers, despite the poem seeming to. It is schematized, declarative, almost cocksure, but full of irreconcilable positions. I want a manifesto that unwrites itself, an antidote for would-be rulers, a poetics that is humble before the community it claims to serve, because, in the end, my right to be heard is nothing other than your right to the same, and so we ought to be listening to each other."

Susan Haldane lives on a farm near the northern boundary of Algonquin Park. Her chapbook *Picking Stones* is published by Gaspereau Press. Her work has been published in a number of Canadian journals and in the anthology *Desperately Seeking Susans* (Oolichan 2012). In 2019 she was thrilled to win the Magpie Award for her poem "A Short History of Space Travel."

Of "Thin-Skinned," Haldane writes, "In early 2018, the news was full of dramatic photos of the eruption of Hawaii's Kilauea volcano, with fissures opening in residential neighbourhoods and lava flowing across roads and into the ocean. At the same time, there seemed to be much earthquake and volcanic activity elsewhere in the world. Despite living thousands of kilometres away from these sites (and on a fairly stable chunk of tectonic plate), this sparked my overactive sense of apocalypse. These are natural processes obviously, but in my mind they combined with all the ways we have hurt and insulted the planet and one another. And I thought about the inadequacy of our attempts at healing, even though we approach these with love."

Louise Bernice Halfe–Sky Dancer was raised on Saddle Lake Reserve and attended Blue Quills Residential School. Louise is married and has two adult children and three grandsons. She graduated with a bachelor's of social work from the University of Regina. She also completed two years of Nechi

Training in St. Albert's Nechi Institute, where she also facilitated the program. She served as Saskatchewan's poet laureate for two years and has traveled extensively. She has served as "keynote speaker" at numerous conferences. Her books, *Bear Bones and Feathers, Blue Marrow, The Crooked Good,* and *Burning In This Midnight Dream,* published by Coteau Books, have all received numerous accolades and awards. *Sôhkêyihta,* her selected poems, was published by Wilfred Laurier Press. Louise was awarded honorary degrees from Wilfred Laurier University and the University of Saskatchewan.

Of "Remember When," Halfe writes, "In Cree and perhaps other Canadian tribal languages we don't have pronouns for the female or male genders. Hence, we use he and she interchangeably and therefore both can appear in one sentence. This may confuse the reader but I am sure the gist will be figured out. We also believe in shapeshifters and that is what awasis is. He can appear as a person or a chosen animal. 'Awasis' in itself means child, but in this case the poem refers to the ADULT-CHILD within. Awasis means glowing sacred flame as we are born with it."

Jane Eaton Hamilton lives near Vancouver. They are the queer, non-binary, disabled author of nine books of creative nonfiction, memoir, fiction and poetry, including *Love Will Burst into a Thousand Shapes.* They have won the CBC Literary Awards in fiction twice and have Notables in *Best American Essays* and *Best American Short Stories.* Their essays appear in places like the *New York Times, The Sun,* and *Gay Magazine* at Medium. In 2020, they won the *EVENT* Non-Fiction contest and second place in the Writer's Digest short fiction contest.

Hamilton writes, "'Game Show' came about after I heard about a Japanese game show where contestants had to guess whether they were looking at, say, a table leg or cake. I couldn't shake the image as a way to process life: had the life I'd been leading been cake, as it seemed to appear to others, or just a single table leg that barely managed to hold up air? I was ruminating about my lost marriage. During the time I was inside it, I pushed down hundreds of instances of abuse, hard and fast, because if I acknowledged even one of them fully, I would have to leave, and I was desperate not to. I had committed to my ex, and my vow meant the world to me. Better and worse. Also, I was disabled, and because I could not seek gainful employment, and because my body needed periodic assistance, it was harder. We had kids. We were complexly intertwined. In a way, I cherished her good side even more because of how terrified I was of her when she hurt me. The good wife was my reward for being able to take on the bad one. The bad one was the price I paid for the compassionate, sweet, exciting woman everyone else saw, and whom I saw, too, most of the time. There were dozens, maybe hundreds, of late nights, covered in bruises, asking myself *Which person is real? What if the bad wife was actually the real one?*"

Maureen Scott Harris lives in Toronto. She has published *A Possible Landscape, Drowning Lessons* (awarded the 2005 Trillium Book Award for Poetry), and *Slow Curve Out.* With the River Poets she leads poetry walks through Toronto parks. Her essay on the Don River won the 2009 WildCare Tasmania Nature Writing Prize. In 2019 she won the Great Blue Heron Poetry Contest and was runner-up in the Edna Staebler Personal Essay Contest.

Harris writes, "'A Room of My Own' began a few years ago when my brother-in-law sent me a poem by K.D. Miller because, he said, it made him think of my mother. Miller's poem—it might have included the line 'My mother had no room of her own'—compared the speaker's privileged access to her own room to her mother's lack of such space, with tenderness towards the mother and the friction between them. At the time I shrugged away from that tenderness and any thought of writing yet another poem about my mother. Later, reading the poem again, I acknowledged that my mother also had no room of her own. The line 'except the one in her mind' came to me because she did not share her inner life. It led to a small poem that surprised and discomfited me by ending 'I also have that room in me.' I put the poem aside for a few months. When I went back to it, expanding, I added details I remembered from childhood, her actual injunctions and instructions, and my feeling of never being good enough, as well as her remark about the sheep thieves. A few drafts included the line 'How bitter I've been about her withholding,' which I dropped. But it prodded me towards the insight the poem ends on. Now I'm inclined to think the line should have stayed."

Dallas Hunt is Cree and a member of Wapsewsipi (Swan River First Nation) in Treaty 8 territory in Northern Alberta. He has had work published in *The Malahat Review, Arc Poetry Magazine, Canadian Literature,* and *Settler Colonial Studies.* His children's book, *Awâsis and the World-Famous Bannock,* was published by Highwater Press in 2018. His first book of poetry, *CREELAND,* will be published by Nightwood Editions in Spring 2021. He is an assistant professor of Indigenous literature at UBC.

Hunt writes, "The poem 'louise' was written in honour of nicapan, Louise Sound (née Potskin). Louise is an interesting figure in our family history, in that much is made of her diminutive stature, the fact that she had only one eye, and her sternness. Of course, much is made of her generosity and her ability to care for her grandchildren and great-grandchildren as well. I wrote a scholarly article for *Canadian Literature* that grapples with the 'archive' and its elisions (intentional, unintentional, and strategic) and found that much is made of my great-grandfather, August Sound, but comparatively little exists in 'official' archival records of my great-grandmother (this absence is typical of Canada and the narratives it likes to tell of itself, as well as the general erasure of Indigenous women, queer, and Two-Spirit peoples from settler, and often times, Indigenous histories). These figures are and have always been integral to our communities and have often done the work of leading, in intimate and public spaces, and yet receive little praise comparative to 'the great men of [Indigenous and non-Indigenous] history.' This poem is a celebration of my great-grandmother, and the work she did within our family and our community—it is an act of presencing."

Ashley Hynd lives on The Haldimand Tract. Her writing grapples with the erasure of her history, both as an act of reclamation and a call of accountability for what has been lost. She was consecutively longlisted for the CBC Poetry Prize (2018, 2019), shortlisted for *Arc Poetry Magazine*'s Poem of the Year (2018), and won the Pacific Spirit Poetry Prize (2017). Ashley is a poetry mentor with Textile KW and sits on the editorial board for both *Canthius Literary Journal* and *Textile KW*.

Hynd writes, "'The Process of Growth' was written in a response to many converging moments, the last of which being my experience of seeing *Every. Now. Then: Reframing Nationhood* at the AGO on Canada Day 150. Writing has always been a visceral process for me, and as I moved through the exhibition, I was constantly writing micro poems in the notes app on my phone. I had already had an idea about writing a sequence poem following the various stages of plant growth, and when I typed up everything from that day, I realized that those micro poems would be the perfect foundation for that piece. They were all written either in response to a piece of artwork or to an interaction with people from that day, they had a central theme around identity and belonging, and they all left something wanting when standing on their own. So, I pasted them into the same Word document and began playing with their arrangement in relation to one another. Eventually I found an order I liked, adding a few other micro poems (from different events) that fit the theme. This poem is fairly unique for me in the sense that it went through several drafts even while being submitted places; the version that was longlisted for the

Pacific Spirit Poetry Prize in 2017 was very different than the one that got published in *Malahat* and appears in this book."

Babo Kamel is originally from Montreal and now resides in Florida. Her work is published in literary reviews in the US, Australia, and Canada, including *The Greensboro Review*, *Painted Bride Quarterly*, and most recently in *Poet Lore*. She holds an MFA from Warren Wilson's Program for Writers, is a Best of the Net nominee, and a six-time Pushcart nominee. Her chapbook, *After*, is published with Finishing Line Press. Find her at: babokamel.com

Of "It's Always Winter When Someone Dies," Kamel writes, "This poem arose from a dream I had a long time ago. In the dream my mother died and left footprints in the snow. The dream continued with each family member dying one by one and leaving similar footprints. When it was my turn, I knew to look for my father's footprints and to place my own feet in them. These images remained with me for years before I attempted to write the poem. Revised many times, it retains very little of the first drafts. Although both of my parents actually died during early winter months, the title attempts to capture the emotional state of grief. Sometimes I am haunted by an image and have to wait for life to catch up to help me understand its significance."

Conor Kerr is a Métis educator, writer, and harvester. Raised in Buffalo Pound Lake, Saskatchewan, his family is descended from the Lac Ste. Anne & Fort Des Prairies Métis communities. Conor is Manager of Indigenous Relations & Supports at NorQuest College and a sessional instructor in the pimâci-hisowin program at MacEwan University. He is the recipient of *The Fiddlehead*'s 2019 Ralph Gustafson Award in poetry. Conor spends most of his time trying to interpret magpie and wrestling labradors.

Kerr writes, "'Directions to the Culture Grounds' was written as a juxtaposition between settler/colonial and Indigenous attitudes towards communication. I've always found solace and comfort in being guided by Elders. I tried to write in the cadence of language and how Elders communicate by interweaving story and connection to land. There's a beauty within the way this relationship is explored in the Elder's section. Even when it's for something as apparently insignificant as giving directions. This poem was born out of the frustration I felt and continue to feel while working within Western systems (children's services, education) that continually devalue Indigenous knowledge while at the same time claiming that they're supporting it. But then to contradict that frustration there's a lot of hope and humour for future generations that's carried within the weight of the Elder's directions. On a literal level (social worker) this is simply directions to a place. But, when you look into it, it's really directions on how to live your life based on kinship, relationality, and a recognition that the land is alive around us. It reminds me that I am always welcome."

Don Kerr is a Saskatoon author who has had published nine books of poetry. Long ago he was one of the first editors of *Grain*. He tries to write poems that can also be popular as "The Clean Language List" is. His first book, *A New Improved Sky*, was edited and organized by Geoffrey Ursell. He has published nonfiction books on the history of Saskatoon, the history of Saskatchewan's libraries, and the Regina ceramics artist Victor Cicansky; as well as a novel for teens, a collection of short stories, and a number of plays.

Fiona Tinwei Lam lives in Vancouver. She has authored three books of poetry, including her most recent collection, *Odes & Laments*. She edited *The Bright Well: Contemporary Canadian Poems on Facing Cancer*. Her prose and poetry appear in more than thirty-five anthologies, including *The Best of the Best Canadian Poetry in English: Tenth Anniversary Edition*, and *Forcefield: 77 Women Poets of BC*. Her poetry videos have screened at festivals locally and internationally. fionalam.net

Of "Ode to the Potato," Lam writes, "Inspired by Pablo Neruda's *Odes to Common Things* (*Odas Elementales*), I wrote a series of ordinary odes, one of which was about potatoes. I remembered how our family would have potatoes (mashed or scalloped) for special occasions like Thanksgiving, Christmas and Easter while I was growing up. Rice and pasta were relatively easy for my widowed mother to make after a long day at the office—just add water and boil—but potatoes took effort, patience, and time. I'll also never forget how my friend Deborah Campbell requested a side order of mashed potatoes (with no accompaniment) as her main course at the Irish Heather Pub when we were university students. It arrived in a pedestaled pewter dish as if it were the finest caviar. It made us think about the potato's significance during the Irish Potato Famine of 1845-49 (also known as The Great Famine), when one million people died and one million more emigrated from Ireland. When I started a backyard garden, my cousin showed me how easy it was to grow potatoes. I would often ask my young son to harvest them with me. Finding those red-skinned potatoes in the dark, damp soil was like finding treasure."

Natalie Lim is a Chinese-Canadian poet based in Vancouver, BC. She is the winner of the 2018 CBC Poetry Prize and *Room Magazine*'s 2020 Emerging Writer Award, with work published in *Room*, *PRISM international*, *Arc Poetry Magazine*, and elsewhere. She is an unashamed nerd and a believer in good bones, and you can find her on Twitter @nataliemlim.

Lim writes, "Several years ago, I wrote a poem called 'porcelain' about wanting to time travel. At the time, I was going through a period of intense loneliness and isolation and I desperately wanted to skip ahead, to fast forward to a place in my life where I was happy and fulfilled. In 2019, I rediscovered 'porcelain' while looking for inspiration in some of my old works, and I found it funny that my feelings on time travel are now exactly the opposite. 'the science of holding on' was born out of gratitude for all the wonderful people in my life, and also out of a deep fear that they won't stay in my life forever. What would happen if I traveled forward in time, only to find that they were gone? I'm writing from my bedroom against the backdrop of the COVID-19 pandemic, reading this poem for the first time in months; at this moment, appreciating time with the people we love has never felt more urgent. Machines, gadgets, narratives of technology and 'progress'—all of that can wait. The nectarines can wait. Let's focus on being with each other while we still can."

Tanis MacDonald lives in Waterloo, Ontario, and is originally (and always) from Winnipeg. She is the author of six books, including *Mobile: poems* (Book*hug 2019) and her memoir of creative life *Out of Line: Daring to Be an Artist Outside the Big City* (Wolsak and Wynn 2018). Her essays and poems have appeared in journals and anthologies in Canada, the United States, and Ireland.

MacDonald writes, "I've been writing myself back into conversation with the natural world, full of chagrin that I ever invested in a belief that I could be separate from it, but thinking too about what kept me believing in that false separation. Being present in the overlapping spaces of the 'urban wild,' that tangle of dependent environments and bodies, is fascinating work, and for me, sometimes it is grief-driven. I have a special interest in creatureliness and the interstices that we make between species and between beings. 'Feeding Foxes' is a much-revised poem with a manic pace: all those strange interrogations mid-poem, all those animal bodies, all that cultural ephemera. I hadn't seen a fox in the wild for years when I wrote this poem, and I thought of the fox that Francis Alÿs released into London's National Portrait Gallery in 2004, videotaping the fox's journey as his piece 'The Nightwatch.' No harm came to the fox, who trotted through the gallery, sniffed a few of the artworks, and found a soft spot to sleep."

Nyla Matuk lives in Toronto. She is the author of two books, *Sumptuary Laws* and *Stranger*, and the editor of *Resisting Canada: An Anthology of Poetry* (Véhicule Press, 2019). She was a finalist for the Gerald Lampert Award and the *Walrus* Poetry Prize, and her poems have appeared in *The Walrus, The New Yorker, Poetry, The Poetry Review, PN Review, The Fiddlehead,* and other magazines in Canada, the UK, and the US. Her work has been included in *New Poetries VI, The Next Wave,* and *Best Canadian Poetry 2012,* among other anthologies. She is the recipient of a Yaddo fellowship and the Mordecai Richler Writer in Residence, McGill University.

Matuk writes, "I wrote 'News Today' as a rumination on newsfeeds: a marine metaphor drawing attention to the murky distinctions between eyewitness accounts and conjecture or opinion, or state propaganda and events as they unfold. I hope the poem draws attention to the volatile nature of ideas in the so-called 'age of information' where history is manipulated conveniently and often."

Sadie McCarney lives in Charlottetown. Her first poetry book, *Live Ones,* came out in Fall 2019 from the University of Regina Press and was longlisted for the Gerald Lampert Memorial Award. A UK/European edition of *Live Ones* was released by tall-lighthouse in Spring 2020. Sadie's work has appeared in publications including *The Walrus, Literary Review of Canada, Grain, The Malahat Review, CV2, The Puritan,* and *EVENT.*

Of "Bee Funeral," McCarney writes, "This poem adds the gloss of years to a real event: my childhood best friend and I really did find a dead bumblebee outside of our neighbourhood rec centre one sweltering summer. We really staged its funeral and gave it grave goods. Everything else, like the catastrophic tone given to the puberty of a best friend who could have been more, was overlaid onto the scene 'in post,' as they say, once I hit my mid-twenties and started writing intently about childhood. The box of crud was a real thing my friend and I called 'The Weird Box,' where we hoarded small items we deemed strange or extraordinary in some way. I hope 'Bee Funeral' fits the criteria for being put in The Weird Box. I hope I do, too."

Tara McGowan-Ross is an urban Mi'kmaq multidisciplinary artist. She is the author of *Girth* (2016) and *Scorpion Season* (Insomniac Press, 2019*).* She lives in Montreal, by way of Halifax, by way of rural Ontario, by way of Toronto. When she is not planting trees she is writing criticism of experimental and independent Montreal theatre, hosting Drawn and Quarterly's Indigenous Literatures Bookclub, and managing the Concordia Community Solidarity Co-Operative Bookstore. Follow her @girthgirl

Of "a simple instruction," McGowan-Ross writes, "In the spring of 2018, I was planting trees in British Colombia. I was not as good as the other veteran planters and I was extremely insecure about it. I wanted to impress my foreman, who we all called Daddy. Daddy pointed out the landmark that defined the edge of my piece for the day: shadows in a cluster of black spruce. He told me 'cut towards the darkness in the forest' and then left me alone for nine hours. Walter Benjamin once wrote that 'the more circumspectly you delay writing down an idea, the more maturely developed it will be on surrendering itself.' I love planting trees. I have learned to be curious about the ways that my tired body conspires with my brain to tell me stories about why planting another tree is impossible. This poem is about the things that came up that day: my insecurity, my grief, my frustration, about colonialism and having my name mispronounced and the long stretches of silence. I think this poem functions like a rap: it is sensationalized, exaggerated, semi-autobiographical fiction. In that clearcut, outrunning insects, managing the terrain and the elements, avoiding carnivorous beasts and despair and other dangers, I daddied myself by imagining the perfect pep talk. Then I went back to my tent and didn't write it. I didn't write it for months, feeling it coming back like a wave, or a nightmare. When it was time, it came out fully formed."

Erín Moure lives in Montreal. Her latest book is *The Elements* (Anansi 2019). In 2020, two new translations: a sequence of Argentinian poet Juan Gelman's "translations" of *John Wendell, Sleepless Nights Under Capitalism* (Eulalia Books) and, from the Galician of Uxío Novoneyra, *The Uplands, Book of the Courel* (Veliz Books). Next up: a translation of Chantal Neveu's *This Radiant Life* (Book*hug) and *Toots fait la Shiva, avenue Minto* (Noroît, tr. Colette St-Hilaire from *Sitting Shiva on Minto Avenue*, by Toots (New Star 2017).

Moure writes, "I wrote 'Odiama' in 2016 in one long sweep after re-reading CD Wright's poem 'from The Obscure Lives of the Poets' from her 2016 posthumous book *Shall Cross*. The poem just energized me and filled me up with oxygen and I missed CD a lot (she'd died early that year) and I felt the vital presence of my lifelong protector and guide, my maternal grandmother, who came to Canada in 1929 via Cleveland (thus the Cayahoga river . . . my grandpa worked for River Furnace making pig iron there) via a return to Ukraine then to Canada as the US had closed its borders. My obscure life would be even more obscure if it weren't for my grandmother. Odiama is when two people merge into one, like blood sisters, you high-five and cry out 'Odiama!' This poem is my high-five. I read CD Wright's poem and looked up and realized I was wearing my grandmother's face. Odiama!"

Roger Nash is inaugural Poet Laureate of the City of Sudbury, and a past president of the League of Canadian Poets. Literary awards include the Canadian Jewish Book Award for Poetry and the PEN/O. Henry Prize Story Award. His latest collection of poetry is *Climbing A Question* (Aeolus House, 2019). He's had twenty books published, in Canada and the UK (poetry, short stories, literary criticism, philosophy). He's professor emeritus at Laurentian University, in environmental ethics.

Nash writes, "'Stutters' opens a sequence of poems in my latest book, *Climbing A Question*. The sequence wrestles with the paradox of how, in the careful words of poetry, we can nevertheless testify to breakdowns in language of various sorts. There are stutters, being bafflingly stuck for the right word, frequent gaps in the sentences of friends with Alzheimer's. So much that nudges us forward in life can seem beyond clear articulation. Shouldn't poetry be a witness to this? For me, more generally, wrestling with paradoxes, of one kind or another, is the very heartbeat of so much important poetry—certainly from John Donne onwards. As it is of key moments in our lives. Several of my friends have been life-long stutterers. Is this jail-time in a life-long disability? Or can it achieve an alternate sense of order and gestured eloquence? Can our weaknesses, in the complexities of life, sometimes come to harbour our very strengths? Perhaps we are all, metaphorically, and at our most insightful moments, stuttering though life. I wrestle with that paradox in the poem."

Samantha Nock is a Cree-Métis writer and podcast host from northeast BC, though her family originally comes from Ile-a-la-Crosse, Saskatchewan. Samantha is currently located on the unceded territories of the Squamish, Tsleil-Waututh, and Musqueam peoples, where she co-organizers and hosts a bimonthly poetry reading series called Poetry is Bad For You. She is also producer and host of Heavy Content, a podcast exploring fat representation in the media. Sam has been published in *Canadian Art, SAD Mag, VICE, PRISM international,* amongst others.

Samantha writes, "I wrote "pahpowin" after reading alongside Dallas Hunt and Billy-Ray Belcourt for the Vancouver launch of Billy-Ray's first book, *This Wound is a World*. The reading had some Big Treaty 8 Prairie energy, and the laughter we shared was like a taste of home. It reminded me of the resilience and power that happens when prairie kin share our loud prairie cackles together. There is nothing more beautiful than the sound of Crees laughing together, there's also no sound louder. I wrote this love poem to loud prairie cackles and the worlds that open up when we laugh together."

Erin Noteboom lives in Kitchener, Ontario. She was trained as a particle physicist but gave it up for a career writing poetry and children's novels. Against the odds, this worked out well. Erin's poetry has won the CBC Literary Award and has twice been shortlisted for the National Magazine Award. She is the author of two volumes of poetry, both from Wolsak & Wynn. Her five novels for younger readers are published under her married name, Erin Bow. The most recent, *Stand On The Sky*, took this year's Governor General's Award in children's literature.

Noteboom writes, "'light/cage' is part of a collection that I'm working on about science and scientists. It's written within the rough cage of a sonnet, and I indulged in a bunch of enjambed rhymes and alliteration to give the poem a stiffer structure than I usually use. I needed the structure to contain a big idea that my science poems keep returning to: the sadness that seems to shadow knowledge. As a kid I imprinted like a duckling on Carl Sagan's *Cosmos*, falling in awestruck love with the beauty of the universe as seen through the lens of science. I studied physics and work as a science writer, and still feel this peculiar joy. But somewhere I also imprinted on Robert Oppenheimer, who became the subject of the first poem I wrote worth keeping. Like the joy, that peculiar haunting has stayed. I have fused sand from the Trinity atomic bomb test site on the wall of my writing office. It's beautiful. In my science-centric collection, I've written about the ship designer Thomas Andrews, who was aboard the Titanic; about Marie Curie holding a vial of radium to her temple to see the flashes in her eyes; about the botanists who protected their seed bank during the siege of Leningrad though they themselves starved. 'light/cage' is different because it gives the knowledge and its twin weights of beauty and sorrow not to any particular scientist, but to all of us."

Abby Paige is originally from northern Vermont and currently lives in New Brunswick. A writer and performer, her work has appeared in publications including *Arc Poetry Magazine*, *Room Magazine*, *Montreal Review of Books*, *Bitch Magazine*, and various anthologies. Her chapbooks are *Clean Margins*, winner of the 2020 Harbor Review Editor's Prize, and *Other Brief Discourses*, published by Ottawa's above/ground press in 2013. Her plays, *Piecework: When We Were French* and *Les filles du quoi?*, explore the legacy of French-Canadian immigration to the United States and are forthcoming from the University of Maine Press.

Paige writes, "Hoems are very short poems on domestic themes: housekeeping, child-rearing, marriage, and other private labours. Those selected here are part of a larger collection that I began when my son was just a few months old and my days were broken into useless fragments. My writing practice felt similarly splintered, and reading poetry at that time, I was struck by how little of my daily life was reflected in what I read. No one made sandwiches in poems, or cleaned toilets or did laundry or bought groceries. Were we not supposed to write about these things? Aside from the obvious practical limits on my writing (I was never alone and always exhausted; interruptions were constant; my desk was sometimes covered in stuffed animals), I began to wonder whether my work was stalled because of my own thinking about what poetry was supposed to be. These tiny poems were how to I tried to reconcile my writing with the reality of my days. I wanted to imagine a poetry that wasn't trying to elevate the domestic, but that would embody the smallness, isolation, monotony, and sometimes absurdity of house-and care-work."

Geoff Pevlin is a poet and innkeeper from the mauzy shores of St. John's, Newfoundland. He also draws, designs, photographs, edits, films, and codes various things. Check out his work at GeoffPevlin.com

Pevlin writes, "'clumper crackies' is based on a true story as told by the Arctic mariner Captain Robert Bartlett of Brigus, Newfoundland, who is also my great-great uncle. In 1913–1914, Bartlett's ship, the *Karluk*, got jammed in heavy ice north of Alaska and floated far off course into a mostly unexplored region north of Siberia. The *Karluk* eventually sank, and Bartlett and his crew lived on a sheet of ice for months. When the weather cleared, the captain and a crew-mate, Kataktovick, trekked seven hundred miles over raftering sea ice and through Siberia to mount a rescue mission from Alaska. The language in this poem is a hybrid of standard and Newfoundland English. All of the non-standard words and expressions are real, and most can be found in the *Dictionary of Newfoundland English*. The poem contains two versions which act as 'translations' of each other. If you don't understand one part of the poem, look to the other version for guidance (for example, a *clumper* is a floating ice pan and a *cracky* is a small dog. So *clumper crackies* translates to ice pan puppies.) 'clumper crackies' is part of a manuscript which tells the story of the ill-fated *Karluk* expedition, tentatively titled *Cramp-Hand Cuffers: The Robert Bartlett Explorations*."

Alycia Pirmohamed is from Alberta, Canada. She is the author of two chapbooks, *Faces that Fled the Wind* (BOAAT Press) and *Hinge* (ignitonpress). In 2019, Alycia won the CBC Poetry Prize. Recently she was also the winner of the *Gulf Coast* Poetry Prize, the *Ploughshares* Emerging Writer's Contest, and the 92Y Discovery Poetry Contest. Alycia is currently a PhD student at the University of Edinburgh, and she received her MFA from the University of Oregon.

Pirmohamed writes, "I wrote 'Avian Circulatory System' as a way to articulate feelings of belonging and un-belonging. The poem does this primarily through imagery that is rooted in the senses, imagery that explores both literal and imagined landscapes. How do you imagine a place you have never visited, yet holds so much of your history? Much of my work is an attempt to weave together various aspects of my cultural heritage and identity. In this poem, I meditate specifically on the body: on inheritance and bloodlines, on the heart and all its connotations, and finally, toward the end of the poem, on the racialised body. In 'Avian Circulatory System,' I want to create imaginative dimensions where all these challenging and complex narratives and histories might reside—but, I also want to capture what is rich and beautiful about all the unique places I call home."

Jana Prikryl is the author of *No Matter* (Tim Duggan Books, 2019) and *The After Party* (Tim Duggan Books, 2016). Born in the former Czechoslovakia, she was a child when her family immigrated to Canada. Her work has received support from the Guggenheim Foundation, the Radcliffe Institute for Advanced Study, and the Canada Council for the Arts. She is a senior editor and the poetry editor at *The New York Review of Books*.

Prikryl writes, "This poem is from my latest book, *No Matter*, which includes six other poems also titled 'Waves.' They are scattered through the collection and aren't a series, exactly—sites of incessant return. In *No Matter*, which taken together is something like an elegy for New York City, these poems might represent the sea and rivers that surround Manhattan—the forces that make us vulnerable: time and the material stuff of our bodies. This particular 'Waves' is the only one of the seven set (to some degree) on firm land. Much of it was first drafted fifteen years ago, only a few years after I moved from Toronto to New York, and to me it's permeated with my earliest feelings about this place."

Jason Purcell lives in Edmonton. He is the author of *A Place More Hospitable* (Anstruther Press, 2019) and co-editor of *Ten Canadian Writers in Context* (University of Alberta

Press, 2016). Alongside Matthew Stepanic, he is co-founder of Edmonton's Glass Bookshop.

Purcell writes, "This poem comes from a series of ekphrastic pieces I'm working on based on the paintings of Kris Knight. Knight, a gay artist based in Toronto, paints portraits of men that are delicate and intimate, and which convey melancholy and sensuality in equal measure. His work makes visible the tension of gay sexual life: while his subjects may appear chaste and soft—pastel colours, gentle poses—they are always already marked by an irrefutable sexuality. There is a sense that the subjects of Knight's work guard themselves against the sexualizing cultural gaze that falls on gay men. I read into these portraits an anxiety around sex and desire, perhaps even a fear of it, and I use *The Flying Monkey* to access this particular anxiety. The shirtless blue boy of Knight's painting, standing in front of blue floral wallpaper, looks down, perhaps in shame or regret. I am interested in this painting's imagery, of the flower—the plant's reproductive structure—drawn around the downturned eye of a boy who is almost disappearing against his backdrop. What does it mean to wish away one's desire?"

Armand Garnet Ruffo is an Anishinaabe writer from remote northern Ontario who currently teaches at Queen's University. He is the author of *Norval Morrisseau: Man Changing Into Thunderbird* (finalist for a Governor General's Literary Award), *The Thunderbird Poems* (finalist for The Raymond Souster Award) and *Treaty #* (finalist for a Governor General's Literary Award). Author of numerous publications, his work appeared in *The Best of The Best Canadian Poetry* (Tightrope Books, 2017).

Ruffo writes, "'Pink Mints' came about quite by accident. I was nearing the completion of my last book *Treaty #* and had submitted a poem to the publisher that was essentially the bones of 'Pink Mints.' In other words, some of the elements of 'Pink Mints' were there, but I still had to get to the heart of it, and yet I was blinded by what was there. One of the problems a poet can encounter is that once the words are on the page they tend to cement themselves together. I'm using the metaphor 'cement' here because it's often difficult to pry the words apart and actually see the poem for what it is or is not. Fortunately, in this case, Paul Vermeersch, my editor at Wolsak & Wynn, pointed out that the original poem just didn't feel finished. It was lacking something. I think it was that very evening I jackhammered the piece apart and started again. I suppose by then I had the distance to ask myself, what am I *really* getting at here? What is the poem *really* about? Once I got back down to that level, it nearly wrote itself. The poem was so different in the end that I even changed the title. Miigwech Paul."

Rebecca Salazar (she/they) is a writer, editor, and community organizer currently living on the unceded territory of the Wolastoqiyik people. The author of poetry chapbooks *the knife you need that justifies the wound* (Rahila's Ghost) and *Guzzle* (Anstruther), Rebecca also edits for *The Fiddlehead* and *Plenitude* magazines. Her first full-length collection is forthcoming in 2021 with McClelland & Stewart.

Salazar writes, "'Poem for unwilling mothers' began as a completely different, much more optimistic poem. Sometime in 2015, I read Raoul Fernandes' poem 'Books for the new child,' in which a parent imagines the stories they will tell a newborn as they grow. The first versions of my poem tried to emulate that tenderness toward a hypothetical child, but felt dishonest. It took a pregnancy-related trauma of my own for me to realize what I was writing was less a response to Raoul's loving poem, and more a rage-filled response to the way childbirth and reproduction were imposed upon me as something compulsory since my own childhood. The poem transformed over the next few years to contain that tension between the heteropatriarchal fantasy of parenthood and the potentially fatal body horror of pregnancy, as well as images of dangerous fertility, miscarriage, and abortion. The poem became a history of what has been done to or by unwilling mothers to suppress or survive ourselves. I still feel grateful to 'Books for the new child' for its affectionate portrayal of willing parenthood and love with full agency, but 'Poem for unwilling mothers' was what I needed to write against a history of non-consent and coercion. It became a spell to channel the anger, grief and power that come with choosing life without parenthood."

Robyn Sarah has lived for most of her life in Montreal. The author of eleven collections of poems, two collections of short stories, and a book of essays on poetry, she served from 2011 to 2020 as poetry editor for Cormorant Books. Her tenth poetry collection, *My Shoes Are Killing Me*, won the Governor General's Award for poetry in 2015, and in 2017 Biblioasis published a forty-year retrospective, *Wherever We Mean to Be: Selected Poems, 1975-2015*.

Sarah writes, "I was amused to be asked for an artist's statement about a poem called 'Artist's Statement,' given that the poem is its own artist's statement, or anti-statement. A refusal to assume an authorial pose, a rejection of group identity as an authorial pose, it's a stubbornly human poem that believes an individual human life can and should speak to, or for, all humanity. I have no recollection of writing this poem. It resurfaced in a file of old unpublished poems when I was looking for something to meet a request to contribute to a magazine, at a time when I had no new work to send. A notebook from the year 2000 tells me I drafted the poem in December of that year, but the genesis seems to have been a month earlier, when I scribbled this note to myself: 'I don't want to write smart or clever or cerebral or even imaginary poems. I want to write sparrow poems'—and, a day or two later: 'Bird tracks / on the surface of snow'—followed by a rough attempt at the first few lines. (What did I mean by sparrow poems? My guess is I was thinking of William Carlos William's 'The Sparrow.' A poem about a bird, but the paradigm is human. It's a wonderful poem; look it up.)"

A settler from Vancouver, **Erin Soros** writes four genres: fiction, nonfiction, poetry, and hybrid scholarly prose. Her stories have won the CBC Literary Award and the Commonwealth Award. An essay in *The Fiddlehead* was a finalist for a National Magazine Award. Her poetry received *The Malahat Review*'s Long Poem Prize and was a finalist for the CBC Literary Award. She is a Postdoctoral Fellow at Cornell University where she researches psychotic responses to complex trauma.

Of "Weight," Soros writes, "This poem cycles through the weight of grief, the weight of trauma, the weight of addiction, the weight of language, the weight of madness—and the opposite, how these things can seem unbearably light. To face these states head-on in the writing felt overwhelming and amorphous, so the return to weight lifting—both literally in my everyday practice and figuratively as a trope in the poem—was a way to create structure and relief. I speak of how rest and repair forms part of the weightlifting regime—the sport demands and enacts recovery. If adolescent self-starvation was paradoxically both a repetition of violence targeted at my embodiment and a painful form of refusal, then weightlifting was one method of returning to physical need as a practice of resistance. Through bracing against pressure, one recreates oneself. When I focus on my own agency—the alphabet of my body, its buoyant energy and brute force—I become more than the victim of someone else's desires. The act of lifting weights unbinds me at least momentarily from gendered norms, or the ones assumed to apply to my frame. Finally I wanted to capture the poetics of muscle and metal: the sweaty, ragged, intimate culture of a gym, the way these men speak and move, not just their strength and sometimes menacing presence, but also their vulnerability, which I have come to witness in both banal and dramatic ways."

Kevin Spenst is the author of *Ignite, Jabbering with Bing Bong* and *Hearts Amok: a memoir in verse* (Anvil Press), and over a dozen chapbooks including *Pray Goodbye* (the Alfred Gustav Press), *Surrey Sonnets* (JackPine Press) and *Upend* (Frog Hollow Press: Dis/Ability series). He teaches creative writing at Vancouver Community College and lives on unceded Coast Salish territory with the love of his life Shauna Kaendo.

Of "It Will Rain Like Rods on the Hillside in Sweden," Spenst writes, "Language is our most electric connection to the past; each word and phrase is a circuit to some point of creation. The idioms from your mother tongue may seem commonplace to you, but when someone is learning your language these same idioms may produce incomprehensibility (how can you really *dig yourself out of a hole*?), amusement, and sometimes a jolt of something poetic. Two winters ago, I tried to wrap my head around the rain in Vancouver; I wrote poems about raindrops, umbrellas, and rainstorms. Having taught English as a second language for over twenty years, the idiom of 'cats and dogs' as rain kept leaping to mind, but then I wondered how other languages describe the rain idiomatically. Through Google searches, expressions from Japanese, German, and other languages started piling up and the frame of a weather-report slowly emerged on the page. While there is an element of light-heartedness to the poem, considering the rise of patriotism around the world, often centered in the purity and inviolability of a national language, I think it's more important than ever to ensure that we keep ourselves open to other sounds, voices, and languages. The existence of languages side by side is not an ugly babble. There are many ways to word the world and the more we bring them together, the more we connect ourselves to a multitude of presents and pasts."

John Elizabeth Stintzi is a non-binary writer who grew up on a cattle farm in northwestern Ontario. In 2019, they were awarded the RBC Bronwen Wallace Award for Emerging Writers from the Writers' Trust of Canada. They are the author of the novel *Vanishing Monuments* (Arsenal Pulp Press) as well as the poetry collection *Junebat* (House of Anansi), and their work has appeared in the *Malahat Review, Kenyon Review, Fiddlehead, Arc Poetry Magazine,* and *Ploughshares.*

Of "Saluations from the Storm," Stintzi writes, "This poem originates from one of those low, dysphoric moments where I feel hopeless in my body—where I feel like my body isn't reflective of who I am as a non-binary person. The poem is both an admonishment of, and an apology to, my body for how estranged I feel by living in it, characterizing the body as a misleading cage because it does not—and possibly may never—effectively communicate who I am to the outside world. This poem arrived almost fully formed when—in one of those dysphoric moments—I found myself acknowledging that while it felt like a cage to me, someone else might be very satisfied to live in my body. This realization led me through the poem to arrive—with some melodrama!—at the declaration that I'd like to see my body happy, which I believed would be possible were it occupied by someone who was a better fit for it."

Andrea Thompson lives in Toronto. She is a poet, novelist, educator, essayist and award-winning spoken word artist who has been publishing and performing her work for over twenty-five years. She is co-editor of the anthology, *Other Tongues: Mixed-Race Women Speak Out,* author of the novel *Over Our Heads,* and creator of the spoken word albums, *One* and *Soulorations.* Thompson teaches through the University of Toronto's continuing studies department, CAMH and Workman Arts. www.andreathompson.ca

Thompson writes, "While studying for my MFA at the University of Guelph, my poetry instructor, Lynn Crosbie, introduced me to the work of Sonia Sanchez—one of the most influential writers in North America. Sanchez was an early advocate of Black studies programs in universities—work that eventually opened the door to the creation of similar programs such as Asian, women's and gender studies.

Sanchez was also a key figure of the Black Arts movement. Her work in the 1960s showed poetry how to use vernacular as a tool for both empowerment and education. The style and formatting of my poem, "To Whyt/Anthology/Editors" was inspired by Sanchez' iconic poem, "to blk/record/buyers"— a call to Black society to support our own artists. The content of my response poem was a cathartic reaction to Joyce Ann Joyce's essay, 'Sonia Sanchez and the African/African-American Literary Tradition: An Anxiety of Confluence,' where Joyce writes: 'African-American writers and poets, such as Sonia Sanchez, remain on the margins of American intellectual history. Nothing testifies to this fact more than Harold Bloom's 1998 edition *The Best of the Best American Poetry: 1988-1997*. This volume contains thirty-three White men, eighteen White women, three Black men, and one Black woman. [...] And even more disturbing is the fact that Sanchez is glaringly omitted from the important *Norton Anthology of Literature by Women* (1984)."

Sanna Wani is a Kashmiri settler, living near the Missinnihe river. She is an MA candidate in Anthropology at the University of Toronto, researching ethnographic poetry, diasporic grief, and oral history. More of her work can be found through her website, sannawani.com. She loves daisies.

Of "As I pray," Wani writes, "This piece was written in my home in Kashmir during the summer of 2018. That home has housed two generations of my family and the house directly behind us, where my paternal grandfather's older brother lives, has housed seven. The poem includes fragments of conversations I had with my parents that summer: about religion, about why they practiced our religion. What I had known from childhood, duty and untouchable tradition, gave way to something more tender and vulnerable in these conversations. In this poem, I wanted to preserve that vulnerability. I wanted to render a space between prayer and conversation around prayer with room for our bodies and the bodies around us, the movements of that summer: everyday habits like going to Nani's house and evening tea in the garden, ordinary features of the land like the rice paddy fields and Zabarwan mountain range. The poem continuously circles back to healing because those conversations (and the poem itself) healed not only the rift between me and my parents but also me and my idea of what faith could be. This intimacy allowed me to reach for prayer again—helped me cherish the ways we could reach for faith together."

Adele Wiseman (1928-1992) was born in Winnipeg. She won the Governor-General's Award in 1956 for her first novel *The Sacrifice*. Her subsequent books included *Old Markets, New World; Crackpot*, winner of the Canadian Booksellers Award; *Old Woman at Play*; and *Memoirs of a Book-Molesting Childhood and Other Essays*. Her poetry, housed in the York University Archives, had been mostly unpublished before a selection appeared in *The Dowager Empress: Poems by Adele Wiseman*, ed. Elizabeth Greene (Inanna, 2019).

Of "Never Put a Poem Off," Elizabeth Greene writes: "When I interviewed Adele's dear friend Arlene Lampert, for *We Who Can Fly: Poems, Essays and Memories in Honour of Adele Wiseman* (Cormorant, 1997), Arlene said, 'I don't know what started [Adele] writing poetry ... I don't know why all of a sudden everything she wanted to say was starting to pop out in poems, and she didn't have an explanation for it.' When I suggested that Adele's poetry was ahead of her time, Arlene said, 'It's totally out of any time. It's not a part of where poetry's going, in a way, and I don't think it ever will be.' Adele's daughter Tamara Stone writes, 'This poem certainly exemplifies her lived philosophy.' 'Never Put a Poem Off' is undated in the archives, but Adele Wiseman's short poetry was written between 1981 and 1986."

NOTABLE POEMS OF 2019

Ken Babstock
"Clotho, Lachesis, Atropos" *The Walrus* July/August 2019

Graeme Bezanson
"I March in the Parade of Liberty but as Long as I Love You I'm Not Free," *PRISM international* Fall 2019

Jenny Boychuk
"Baby Fat," *The New Quarterly* Winter 2019

Dionne Brand
"Verso 47," *Literary Review of Canada* Vol. 27, Issue 1

Heather Cadsby
"Shoulder Replacement: metal ball and plastic socket," *Juniper Poetry* Vol. 3, Issue 1

Weyman Chan
"Pick Me Up," *The Malahat Review* Issue 208, Autumn 2019

Alexei Perry Cox
from "Finding Places to Make Places," *Vallum* 16.2 Fear

Rachel Crummey
"An Exhibition Concerning the Life and Death", *Maisonneuve* 71 Spring 2019

Timiro Mohamed
   "Orchestra," *PRISM international* Spring 2019

A.F. Moritz
   "Allegory of the Wind," *Contemporary Verse 2* Winter 2019 Vol. 41, No. 3

Daniel David Moses
   "How a Turtle Rattles," *Grain* 46.5 Summer 2019

Sahar Muradi
   "Excerpts from Night Nursing," *Arc Poetry Magazine* Fall 2019

Shane Neilson
   "Deep Religious Faith," *The Walrus* January/February 2020

Hoa Nguyen
   "Crow Pheasant," *Vallum* 16.1 Connections

Natalie Rice
   "Bowline," *EVENT* 48.1

Autumn Richardson
   "An Almost-Gone Radiance," *EVENT* 48.1

Angelina Schellenberg
   "Dear Raspberry Patch," *Juniper Poetry* Vol. 3, Issue 1

Michelle Speyer
   "unwritten letters," *The Trinity Review* 131 Spring 2019

waaseyaa'sin Christine Sy
   "Ikawe (Not) on the Land," *Grain* 46.5 Summer 2019

Rob Taylor
   "The Baffled King," *Juniper Poetry* Vol. 3 Issue 1

Sarah Tolmie
   "58," *Literary Review of Canada* Vol. 27, No. 5

Jade Wallace
   "Rituals of Sanction," *Canthius* Issue 07

Catriona Wright
   "Seasonal Affective Disorder," *The Walrus* January/February 2020

Sarah Yi-Mei
   "Worms," *Vallum* 16.2 Fear

Banoo Zan
   "My Labor and My Leisure," *Arc Poetry Magazine* Fall 2019

MAGAZINES CONSULTED

Each year, the fifty best poems and the list of notable poems by Canadian poets are selected from more than fifty print and online journals published in the previous year. While direct submissions of individual poems are not accepted, we welcome review copies from print outlets and announcements of new issues from online publications. Please direct two copies of each print issue to Best Canadian Poetry c/o Biblioasis, 1686 Ottawa St, Ste 100, Windsor, ON N8Y 1R1, or email us at bestcanadianpoetry@biblioasis.com.

The Antigonish Review (antigonishreview.com). PO Box 5000, Antigonish, NS, B2G 2W5
Arc Poetry Magazine (arcpoetry.ca). PO Box 81060, Ottawa, ON, K1P 1B1
Brick, A Literary Journal (brickmag.com). PO Box 609, Stn. P, Toronto, ON, M5S 2Y4
Bywords (bywords.ca)
Canadian Broadcasting Corporation, CBC Poetry Prize finalists (cbc.ca)
Canadian Literature (canlit.ca). University of British Columbia, 8–6303 NW Marine Dr., Vancouver, BC, V6T 1Z1

Canadian Notes & Queries (notesandqueries.ca).1686 Ottawa
    St., Suite 100, Windsor, ON N8Y 1R1.

Canthius (canthius.com)

The Capilano Review (thecapilanoreview.ca). 102-281 Indus-
    trial Ave., Vancouver, BC, V6A 2P2

Carousel (carouselmagazine.ca). UC 274, University of Guelph,
    Guelph, ON, N1G 2W1

Carte Blanche (carte-blanche.org)

Cascadia Rising Review (cascadiarisingreview.com)

Contemporary Verse 2 (*CV2*) (contemporaryverse2.ca). 502–
    100 Arthur St., Winnipeg, MB, R3B 1H3

Cosmonauts Avenue (cosmonautsavenue.com)

Dalhousie Review (dalhousiereview.dal.ca). Dalhousie Uni-
    versity, Halifax, NS, B3H 4R2

Dusie (dusie.org)

EVENT (eventmagazine.ca). PO Box 2503, New Westminster,
    BC, V3L 5B2

Exile Quarterly (theexilewriters.com). Exile/Excelsior Pub-
    lishing Inc., 170 Wellington St. W, PO Box 308, Mount
    Forest, ON, N0G 2L0

Existere (yorku.ca/existere). Vanier College 101E, York Uni-
    versity, 4700 Keele St., Toronto, ON, M3J 1P3

Feathertale (feathertale.com/review). PO Box 5023, Ottawa,
    ON, K2C 3H3

The Fiddlehead (thefiddlehead.ca). Campus House, Univer-
    sity of New Brunswick, 11 Garland Ct., PO Box 4400,
    Fredericton, NB, E3B 5A3

filling Station (fillingstation.ca). PO Box 22135, Bankers Hall,
    Calgary, AB, T2P 4J5

Forget Magazine (orgetmagazine.com). 810–1111, Melville St.,
    Vancouver, BC, V6E 3V6

Geist (geist.com). Suite 210, 111 W. Hastings St., Vancouver,
    BC, V6B 1H4

Glass Buffalo (glassbuffalo.com). HC 3–59, Humanities Build-
    ing, University of Alberta, 116 St. and 85 Ave., Edmon-
    ton, AB, TG6 2R3

Grain (grainmagazine.ca). PO Box 3986, Regina, SK, S4P 3R9

HA&L (Hamilton Arts & Letters Magazine) (halmagazine. wordpress.com)

Juniper Poetry (juniperpoetry.com)

The Leaf (brucedalepress.ca). PO Box 2259, Port Elgin, ON, N0H 2C0

Lemon Hound (lemonhound.com)

The Literary Review of Canada (reviewcanada.ca). *340 King St E, Toronto, ON M5A 1K8*

Maisonneuve (maisonneuve.org). 1051 boul. Decarie, PO Box 53527, Saint Laurent, QC, H4L 5J9

The Malahat Review (malahatreview.ca). University of Victoria, PO Box 1700, Stn. CSC, Victoria, BC, V8W 2Y2

Maple Tree Literary Supplement (mtls.ca). 1103–1701 Kilborn Ave., Ottawa, ON, K1H 6M8

The Maynard (themaynard.org)

Minola Review (minolareview.ca)

New Poetry (newpoetry.ca)

The New Quarterly (tnq.ca). St. Jerome's University, 290 Westmount Rd. N, Waterloo, ON, N2L 3G3

ottawater (ottawater.com)

Poetry Is Dead (poetryisdead.ca). 5020 Frances St., Burnaby, BC, V5B 1T3

Prairie Fire (prairiefire.ca). 423–100 Arthur St., Winnipeg, MB, R3B 1H3

PRISM international (prismmagazine.ca). Creative Writing Program, University of British Columbia, Buchanan Room E462, 1866 Main Mall, Vancouver, BC, V6T 1Z1

The Puritan (puritan-magazine.com)

Queen's Quarterly (queensu.ca/quarterly). Queen's University, 144 Barrie St., Kingston, ON, K7L 3N6

Ricepaper (ricepapermagazine.ca). PO Box 74174, Hillcrest RPO, Vancouver, BC, V5V 5L8

Riddle Fence (riddlefence.com)

Room (roommagazine.com). PO Box 46160, Stn. D, Vancouver, BC, V6J 5G5 *subTerrain* (subterrain.ca). PO Box 3008, MPO, Vancouver, BC, V6B 3X5

Taddle Creek (taddlecreekmag.com). PO Box 611, Stn. P, Toronto, ON, M5S 2Y4

The / temz / Review (thetemzreview.com)

This Magazine (this.org). 417–401 Richmond St. W, Toronto, ON, M5V 3A8

Understory (understorymagazine.ca). RR#1, Lunenburg, NS, B0J 2C0

Vallum (vallummag.com). 5038 Sherbrooke W., PO Box 23077, CP Vendome, Montreal, QC, H4A 1T0

The Walrus (walrusmagazine.com). 411 Richmond St. E., Suite B15, Toronto, ON, M5A 3S5

West End Phoenix (westendphoenix.com). The Gladstone Hotel, 1214 Queen St. W., Toronto, ON, M6J 1J6

INDEX TO POETS

ACKNOWLEDGEMENTS

"Artist's Statement" appeared in *Juniper* copyright © 2019 Robyn Sarah. Reprinted with permission of the author.

"As I pray" appeared in *Canthius* copyright © 2019 Sanna Wani. Reprinted with permission of the author.

"Avian Circulatory System" appeared in *The Fiddlehead* copyright © 2019 Alycia Pirmohamed. Reprinted with permission of the author.

"Bee Funeral" appeared in *Literary Review of Canada* copyright © 2019 Sadie McCarney. Reproduced from *Live Ones* (Oskana Poetry & Poetics at the University of Regina Press, 2019) by permission of the author and publisher.

"Blockade" appeared in *The G oose* copyright © 2019 Rob Budde. Reprinted with permission of the author.

"The Clean Language List" appeared in *Grain* copyright © 2019 Don Kerr. Reprinted with permission of the author.

"clumper crackies/Ice Pan Puppies" appeared in *The Fiddlehead* © 2019 Geoff Pevlin. Reprinted with permission of the author.

EDITOR BIOGRAPHIES

Marilyn Dumont is of Cree/Métis ancestry, her Dumont family having lived in the Edmonton area which has a rich Métis historical and contemporary presence. Poet, writer, and professor, Marilyn Dumont teaches with the Faculty of Native Studies and the Department of English and Film Studies at the University of Alberta. Her four collections of poetry have all won either provincial or national poetry awards: *A Really Good Brown Girl* (1996); *green girl dreams Mountains* (2001); *that tongued belonging* (2007); and *The Pemmican Eaters* (2015). She was awarded the 2018 Lifetime Membership from the League of Canadian Poets for her contributions to poetry in Canada, and in 2019, she was awarded the Alberta Lieutenant Governor's Distinguished Artist Award.

Amanda Jernigan is a poet, editor, essayist, librettist, and play-maker. She is the author of three books of poems: *Groundwork* (Biblioasis, 2012), *All the Daylight Hours* (Cormorant Books, 2014), and *Years, Months, and Days* (Biblioasis, 2018)—the last of these named a best book of the year in the *New York Times*. She works as a professor of creative writing and English literature at Saint Mary's University in K'jipuktuk/Halifax.

Anita Lahey's latest book is *The Last Goldfish: a True Tale of Friendship* (Biblioasis, 2020). She's also author of the Véhicule Press poetry collections *Out to Dry in Cape Breton* and *Spinning Side Kick*, and the prose collection *The Mystery Shopping Cart: Essays on Poetry and Culture* (Palimpsest, 2013). Anita is a past editor of *Arc Poetry Magazine* and has served as series editor of *Best Canadian Poetry* since 2018, and prior to that was BCP's assistant series editor since 2014. She lives in Ottawa, on unceded Alongonquin, Anishinabek territory.